WHAT HAPPENS WHEN YOU
DIE

WHAT HAPPENS
WHEN YOU
DIE

An Inside Look At The Ever-Growing Death Industry

A.L. EDWARDS

PALMETTO
P U B L I S H I N G
Charleston, SC
www.PalmettoPublishing.com

Hardcover ISBN: 979-8-8229-3785-7
Paperback ISBN: 979-8-8229-3786-4
eBook ISBN: 979-8-8229-3787-1

Dedicated to my wonderful family who always stands by me no matter how maniacal I can be. Also dedicated to the people in this industry who still have not lost sight of what it means to be there for families and to take pride in a craft.

A.L.

Contents

Foreword

For almost fifteen years, I worked in the funeral industry. It was a job, when I needed a job and there is no doubt in my mind, to this very day, that I learned much in my tenure as a death care professional. I worked with some people whom I feel, were skilled artisans and caring funeral professionals. I also experienced the opposite side of that spectrum, working with and coming to know some of the most scatterbrained and quite frankly moronic people that God ever placed on this earth.

I left the industry in the spring of 2023 and regret nothing about my exit. But before going further, I must let you know that this is in no way a literary middle finger to my past employer. Nor is this a hatchet job on the funeral industry as a whole. Instead, I view these words that I present to you as a cautionary tale. A story of what happens when you or a hospice nurse makes that late night phone call to that funeral establishment because your husband, brother, grandmother, child or whomever has just taken their last breath. On many a website belonging to funeral homes all over the country, there is a little link that you click on. The link is titled, "A Death Has Occurred, What Is Next?" You click on this link and you are liable to get any type of information. But really it comes down to, someone has died and it's time to make their arrangements, whether that be cremation, burial, scientific donation, donor, etc. All in all, the funeral home's website on which you are on, wants to be involved. Why? To make money, of course. But it is done so all in the name of "providing an important service to families."

You see, if you need a mechanic, you try to find one who won't rip you off, one who will do quality work and not bullshit you. A doctor? You want one you can be honest with and one who will be caring and compassionate. A dog-walker? A babysitter? A restaurant? It really doesn't matter; you want the same from all of these. A reliable, trustworthy professional that offers a good product or service and a fair and reasonable price. You read reviews, go to Google and search out the best fit for you. But when it is a "sudden need" when you get that call from the police late at night because your beloved son or daughter has had an accident that has resulted in their fatality, your research goes out the window and you choose the big fancy funeral home that maybe you have only driven by. Or maybe it's that place that did your Aunt Lottie's funeral and the folks seemed nice. When the need is there, and unexpected, you just don't have a lot of time to think and research.

Let's say you walk into the plushest, swankiest restaurant in town. You walk in as the piano tinkles in the corner. The Maitra d' and wait staff are all dressed impeccably and ready to serve. You are shown to your table and you see that everyone is courteous and professional. Of course, that is "front of house." It doesn't matter how many Michelin stars this place has received, if you go to the "back of house," you see something very different. People shouting orders, curse words flying (ever see Gordon Ramsey?) Entire meals being thrown into the trash or elsewhere and staff going toe to toe and threatening each other to "take it out back" to settle the score. Drama, and bullshit. These things exist everywhere and the funeral industry is not immune to it. Only in the funeral industry, you don't get "do overs." You don't get "oops, my bad." In a funeral home, the stakes are just a bit higher.

I got into this industry as a possible career change. After years of working in the entertainment industry, I was looking for a career where I could serve others and get out of my own ego. I was even seriously considering becoming a licensed funeral director. However, after six months in the business, I opted to not get licensed. In fact, I was tempted to leave altogether. But I stuck it out and soon became one of the best crematory managers in the death care industry.

I say that not to sound self-important or puffed up but because it's true. My numbers speak for themselves, and the multiple funeral homes I cremated for have attested many times to the fact that I got results. I gave them service, respect, and most of all, care for their customer.

The following is a look at the back of the house. The good, the bad, and the ugly. The professionals and the incompetents. Many books have been written about this industry. More often than not, they are written by a very biased and slanted licensed funeral director. There have been humorous anecdotes about family squabbles, stalled hearses, and oopsies like "Aunt Doreen's makeup made her look like a circus clown" or "The headstone was misspelled—my Uncle John's marker read 'Joan,' tee hee."

This book is very different. I am not a licensed funeral director, but I have worked behind the scenes and I now offer an objective view of an industry that everyone must use at some time in their lives. All too often, the choice is made on the fly. Through no fault of the family, of course; it is just the nature of the beast. A death has occurred, a sudden death, a death that no one saw coming.

A decision must be made—now. So you go with an establishment that you have perhaps heard good things about, or you just like the looks of building. You choose these "professionals" to do some event planning of the *final* event. You want professionalism, compassion, and skill. You want people you can trust. Yes, there are those companies out there. Even the one I worked for performed their craft, at times, with dignity and caring. It wasn't all dumpster fires and fuckups. There were some great moments here, and I will make mention of those as well. My aim is to be fair and objective. I still have friends in this industry and the ones I still consider friends are true professionals whom I respect because *they* respect. They have respect for the living and those in their care.

With that said, everything you read here is true. It all happened. The names have been changed to protect the ignorant and to cause no financial hardship to any particular establishment. This is simply an eyes-wide-open view of an industry that maybe you wanted to know about but were afraid to ask, were afraid of but had questions about, or maybe you simply wondered why grandma looked so awful there in her pink coffin. I hold no ill will toward those who gave me a living for fifteen years but do wish many in this business to take a little more care.

This is behind the scenes presented for you. People like steak; they just don't want to know how it gets to the plate. Enjoy.

CHAPTER 1

... the Beginning

The man wearing a pair of shorts and flip-flops, topped off by a white polo shirt looked at me and asked me, "Why do you want to work for a funeral home—morbid curiosity?" I must admit, as many job interviews that I had been through in my forty-one years on the planet, this was the most casual and was capped off by this most unusual question. I responded by admitting I knew little of the job I was applying for. I also admitted that it seemed I had seen my fair share of funeral homes, starting at the age of five when my own father had passed suddenly of a massive heart attack. From there, my childhood, on into adolescents and young adulthood was filled with a parade of funerals. By the time I was twenty-five I had looked down into more caskets of family, friends and loved ones than I had ever anticipated. At five, it was my father; at ten, my cousin, who was my age was hit by a car and killed. My dad's brother, whom I had been close to, passed when I was almost fifteen. In my early twenties my best friend had died from brain cancer, and the list goes on. I was indeed no stranger to funerals.

The man behind the desk was dressed more like a pool boy than a successful owner of two very lucrative funeral homes and now his own crematory. Don had begrudgingly gotten into this business as it was his family business. His father and grandfather were both funeral directors, and Don decided as he got older, he would give it a shot. He became a licensed funeral director and worked for ̄ funeral homes in the area until branching out on his own. He owne̊ the business with his wife, and it had quite a name and reputation in the area as a solid family-owned establishment.

Don proceeded to tell me about the job. He told me that it re-quired one to be dressed in a suit and tie, help with removals (that's picking deceased persons up from their place of death), and working funerals. In a nutshell, I was to help the funeral directors with what-ever they needed me to do. I was also told that there would be nights where I would be on call. I would go sometimes to houses where bodies had been "not found for days" and I would have to deal with smells and some unpleasant circumstances. "You'd be slippin' in their stuff" is how he put it. "Ew," I thought, but out loud I said, "I think I can handle it." After all, what other prospects did I have?

Late in 2008, the day after Christmas to be exact, I had just spent the past eight years working for a top rated 100,000-watt country music radio station as a top-rated radio personality when I was let go. Yep, the day after Christmas, I was fired. Fired from a station where I had truly loved working. I started off working at the station part-time in 2000 to supplement my income from my job with an insurance company. It was great to be working in radio again. That was, after all, my first love. I had gone to broadcasting school after high school and had worked at various stations up north. I had spent about ten years at various stations and finally moved down south to continue my broadcast career. I would work at one station, then the next, then the next, and in between, when stations weren't hiring, I took on a multitude of "grown-up jobs." I worked in sales, pest control, finance, and insurance. Sometimes I would work these jobs *and* have radio gigs on the side. That is how the country station came to be.

I had tried for years to get in at this very popular station, and finally, just at a time when I really needed a second job, they gave me a shot. I got in. I worked overnights and weekends at the radio station and then five days of the week I would be at my "day job" at a large insurance company. Many times, I would do an overnight shift at the station and then go into work at the insurance company and work all day. Looking back, I don't know how I did it. Let's just chalk it up to, I was younger. After about five years as a part-timer, the radio station offered me a full-time slot. Gleefully, I accepted, said goodbye to the insurance company, and got back into my true love—radio—full-time!

But it was not to last. About two years later, I was dismissed. I was a victim of a shitty economy and loss of sponsorship at the station. I was the overnight guy and not really considered a key player, so I got the ax. I received a severance and started to look for other radio work, but it was not to be. Commercial radio was taking a financial hit and stations were laying off all over the country. I was just one more out-of-work DJ. I needed to find another line of work, something, fulfilling, something I would enjoy as much as I did radio. Then I had a thought: death. No, not my own. Things hadn't become *that* bad. More specifically, the funeral profession. Yes, it seems I had a bit of a morbid side to me. I was quite fascinated with death. If anyone in the funeral business tells you that they are not morbid or fascinated with death, they are lying. They *all* are fascinated and intrigued with that time when the heart stops beating and the undertaker comes. I was no different in that regard. I thought, "Perhaps a funeral home is a place I could work."

I had a friend who worked for a time with a local funeral home, and he had a friend who was working as a funeral director for a large firm in the area. I thought, "Hell, I'll give it try." After all, my severance was about to run out and I was in need of a job—any job. Even dealing with dead people sounded plausible. So I met with my friend's friend, Carl. Carl was a nice enough guy and we shared a quirky sense of humor. He showed me around the funeral home and having respect for the dearly departed in their care, spared me the embalming or "prep" room. Carl was all about respect for the dead and I liked that. He forwarded my information to Don, the owner, and later that week, Don called me and had me meet him at the crematory for an interview. I dressed up for the interview, as mentioned previously, Don, did not.

Don had chosen to meet me at the crematory, and it would be the same crematory that years later I would run. In the middle of the interview, Don said, "Come to the back, I have to stoke the fire." We walked to the back area of the facility where this massive oven was. He pushed a button and the door raised open. Sticking a large metal pole into the cavity of the machine, he readjusted the burning corpse inside the unit. I watched with amazement as he performed this task. He looked at me, I hadn't passed out or thrown up, so I guess he figured I could handle the job. He closed the door and we went back into the office and concluded the interview.

I got the job and I was excited, excited that I had perhaps found another career opportunity that offered some security and I could be interested in. Don liked me but told me that I must get rid of my earring (yes, I had a pierced ear) as a condition of working for them. The earring went, and I started on a Thursday and soon got to know all the staff. Carl and Ronald were the two funeral directors who ran one of the locations of the two funeral homes. In the next town over, the two funeral directors were Kenny and Joe. Kenny was the FDIC (funeral director in charge) of that location. Carl was the FDIC of the other. Both men were very similar but very different. Kenny was all about the dollars and cents. How much could he get on a contract? What kind of overpriced casket could he talk the family into? Carl, on the other hand, though not above the sales pitch, had a soft-spoken demeanor and caring attitude that instantly put families at ease. Kenny was more of a carnival barker / used car salesman. "What can I do to put granny in this stainless-steel casket here…low mileage on this one!" OK, that is a bit of an exaggeration, but you get the picture.

To summarize, the funeral directors were Carl and Ronald at Branch B and Kenny and Joe at Branch A. Then there was administrative help. Each funeral home had a female office manager, overseeing finance, paperwork et cetera and at the bottom of the pecking order was the support staff personnel or "unlicensed staff" of which I had just become a part. Their job was to do whatever the funeral directors told them. Everything from picking up the deceased from the hospital, nursing home, hospice center, or residence to helping with embalming, mopping, cleaning, and working funerals and graveside services. The job was diverse. You would literally be scrubbing toilets in the morning and then that afternoon, standing at the front of a packed megachurch beside a casket with hands folded in front of you, nodding and greeting mourners.

I was one of three support staff. One was Kenny's son. If you have ever seen *Forest Gump*, then you know Kenny's son. He was Gump, minus the success story. He was not the sharpest tool in the shed but was strong as an ox and the guy you wanted with you when you needed to get a three-hundred-pound dead guy off the floor of a house.

Then there were two others, Gary, the son of Don, the owner, who came on board about a week after I did. Gary and I worked together quite a bit and we became good friends. Gary was funny, kind-hearted and friendly. But being the son of the owner, he was often called away to work on projects his dad had for him. He also could take a day off on a whim and not really suffer too many consequences for those actions. Couple that with some personal peccadillos and it became clear that nepotism had its benefits.

Lastly, was a man about my age who was working at the funeral home while going to school to become a funeral director. Mark was a nice enough guy and very gung-ho about the business but you could immediately tell, he was not very well-liked because of his pedantic nature. He would later obtain his license but would never really gain the respect of the other funeral directors. To them, he was no longer a peon, just a licensed peon.

Everyone was very welcoming and showed me little tricks of the trade. It was a kind of learn-as-you-earn type of situation and I certainly did learn—a lot. The training was almost nonexistent. Really, more or less, it was common sense and a decent work ethic that dictated your own success. The most challenging obstacle became the personalities. The office personnel of each location were kind of your bosses. You followed directives from them when the funeral directors were otherwise occupied.

Branch B, had an older British lady who personified just about every Disney villain rolled into one. She would snap your head off and would plainly tell you that you were nothing more than a "doer," not a "thinker," and she would have you fired in a heartbeat if you crossed her. Did she have a wardrobe made of Dalmatian fur? I do not know though I had my suspicions.

At Branch A, there was an administrator who had basically done a little bit of everything in the business and knew it back to front. In fact, she was the person to ask if ever in doubt about anything. Very approachable and kind. Polar opposites, these two who worked the office.

Working and living in the South is great. Nice people, great weather, though the heat can be unbearable at times, especially when you are dressed in a black suit, standing by a grave in a cemetery with no shade. The sun is an unforgiving bitch! I swear, I felt like a snow cone in hell at times, melting and dealing with a blistering sunburn on my pasty white face. But I found the work rewarding as I witnessed young children whom had just lost their father or a young girl who had to say goodbye to grandma. Growing up attending funerals, losing those close to you, I could most definitely relate.

I met a lot of great people in this business in a short time but as one who tends to lean left a bit politically and one who does not think in terms of color or race, I found myself in a sort of minority. I soon learned that my superiors, Kenny and Joe were right-wing extremists. Now, you may be asking what this has to do with the funeral biz? The short answer is, everything. There is little room in any business for hatred. Hate affects people. The way they view people, the way they act toward people and in business, the way they will serve those people. In the death-care industry, there is certainly no room for racism and hatred, but there it was, in all its ugly glory.

In the office, the air would turn blue with comments about our African-American then-president, then the talk would turn to vitriolic hatred of the first lady, gay people, teachers, unions, ACLU, Hispanics, and the list goes on. Everything and everyone became fair game. Gays were mentally deranged. Teachers were just people who couldn't face reality and wanted to stay in school forever, all Muslims were terrorists and so on. Rush Limbaugh's show was pumped through a computer every day at noon and the vileness that came from those speakers was soon regurgitated from the mouths of the funeral directors. I soon observed these "gentlemen" making comments and wonder if it would affect the way they treated those who came to them for the care of their loved one. Again, the short answer is, it did.

The N-word was bandied about if there was an African-American decedent in their care. Kenny would even regale you with stories of how one of his uncles was a grand wizard in the KKK. The man would actually brag about this shit. Bigotry and stereotyping were the norm. If someone died tragically of HIV, then assumptions were made about why and how. Some of the comments that were made about homosexuals sickened me. Even when I asked them to stop as I had family I loved and supported who were gay, the comments continued. Basically, it came down to this: If there was a police officer or a well-to-do family that required our services, the red carpet was rolled out. The more money that was paid, the better the service. The better the service, the more money that came into the funeral home. However, if the family was impoverished, or their loved one was a criminal or died of a drug overdose, if it was a suicide or someone who had succumbed to HIV, then the remarks, comments and hatred would abound.

However, there are always exceptions. I mean, I did witness instances where the family had no money and things were taken care of, breaks were given. I saw times where the funeral directors worked very hard to give people a proper burial or help with county assistance for a cremation. But nonetheless, the locker-room talk about how or why someone died or the "nutcase family" they had to contend with would continue. It was very clear that I was alone in a sea of hate-filled, bigoted anger and fear. I found myself trying to ignore these comments as I needed the job and these people were my superiors. But of course, when I say "superior," I mean in employment only. Strong opinions and biases did not just pertain to people of color race or sexual orientation but also of their own industry and how Cremation was being chosen over burial.

It soon became evident that the funeral directors I worked with were not fans of cremation. Don had just purchased the cremator a few months prior to my employment and had it placed at a local industrial park. Kenny and Joe hated cremation. "It was a throw away!" "You don't care what happens to your loved one if you choose cremation! Why Don ever bought that crematory is beyond me!" These were some of the complaints about cremation that took place. The fact of the matter was, in the geographic area we were in, in 2009, cremation made up about 35 percent of dispositions in the funeral industry. Burials, as funeral directors will tell you, are where the real money is. Mark-ups on caskets are unreal, and on average families would pay $8,000–$10,000 for a full-service funeral with embalming, visitation, graveside, the whole enchilada. Whereas cremation through the funeral home was running about $2,000.00. So, again, the real money was in the full-service funeral. It is interesting to note that those number have now flipped. The percentage of cremations in this region is running in the seventies, and the full-service burial is in the thirties.

Now, not all funeral homes own their own cremation equipment. Many funeral establishments "contract" the cremation out to facilities that *do* have the equipment. The funeral home I worked for, had their cremations done by a local crematory until Don thought that the money he was spending having someone else do his cremations could be better spent toward equipment of our own. That way, we could also advertise that we "own our own crematory." It puts the families at ease knowing that their loved one is in one place, start to finish.

In essence, Don and his wife Nancy saw the future. They saw cremation becoming more in demand and they did something about it. Their business would only flourish from their astute observations. No matter what their funeral directors thought or said, cremation was a thing of the future and there was nothing anyone could do to stop it other than adapt and put recourses toward that end.

CHAPTER 2

How Do You Think
They Get There?

"We got a call." Kenny said. It was two thirty in the morning. I was on call so when my phone rang, I knew it was time to work. Kenny met me at the funeral home. He was moving a stretcher and some "necessities" into the plain white van when I pulled in. I got out of my car and said, "Hey, why aren't we taking the removal car?" The funeral home had some really nice GMC removal vehicles. Sleek, black and shiny, these cars were equipped with no back seats but instead, a flat stainless-steel bed with rollers, just right for rolling in stretchers, caskets, et cetera.

"It's a decomp," Kenny said.

"Oh God," I thought

A "decomp" was short for decomposing body. This is an often-used term in the funeral and removal industry. If you have a decomp, you are in for a world of smells, fluids and circumstances deemed quite unpleasant even by those with strong constitutions.

"Do we know how old?" I asked.

What I meant by this was not the age of the person but how long they had been "lying around" until discovered. There are a number of factors that affect the rapidity of decomposition. Is the body in a regular structure or a mobile home? Are they outside? If they are inside, was the air conditioning on? Where in the house are they?

Are they in the bathroom? A bathtub? What do we know? That is what I wanted to know. Just what the hell was I walking into?

Kenny simply grunted, "been dead a while…"

There are funeral homes that will be on a sort of "rotation list." The funeral home that I worked for was on this list. It is a list that local police and sheriff's offices use when a body is "found." It works like this. Neighbors say, "Golly, good goddamned, I ain't seen Johnny Jones in about a week. I ain't seen him outside, his newspapers and mail is piled up. Must be somethin' wrong." So, they call the cops to do a wellness check. That is usually when they find them.

The next call that is made is from the police or sheriff to the medical examiner. They go over the circumstances and look for pill bottles or paperwork with a doctor's name. They lay out the scene for the medical examiner, and if the death is not suspicious—for instance, if it is pretty clear that the person died of natural causes and they have no reason to believe that there was foul play—the medical examiner will reach out to that doctor.

Medical examiner.: Hey Doc, we have a Johnathan Jones who has just been found dead. You were treating Mr. Jones?

Doctor.: Yes, he was in my care for cardio arrythmia and Hypertension.

Medical examiner: Are you willing to sign a death certificate for Mr. Jones?

Doctor.: Yes, I will sign.

Medical examiner: Okee dokey…*not* a medical examiner case. Call the next funeral home on the list.

And that is how *we* get called instead of the medical examiner removal people who would take the body to the examiner's office. Instead, we take the body to the funeral home.

Sometimes, it's a coronary and they are face down in their kitchen and it looks like they died about 2 or 3 that afternoon. Other times hospice is involved, the person has been ill for some time and they have finally peacefully succumbed to whatever illness they had with family at their bedside. Then there are those like the one we were just call on. One where they died about 2 or 3 *weeks* ago and they have just been "discovered."

We get to the house. The police are standing outside—all of them. *That* is *never* a good sign. They point to the house, "Back bedroom, about two or three weeks."

"Aw shit," we both say simultaneously.

Now, if you are squeamish or sicken easily, go to the next chapter. That chapter has puppies and marigolds in it. Butterflies with small children playing and laughing. No, just kidding this whole book is about death and funerals. But this is one of the more gruesome parts of the gig.

There he is. Lying on his back on the bed, hands over his head and certainly very stinky and discolored. Flies are abundant. We had to start swatting them away from our faces the minute we enter. Of course, then there is the byproduct of the flies. Their larvae, otherwise known as maggots. It is not a pretty scene. We walk over to the bed; we briefly discuss how we were going to do this, and we walk outside to get our stretcher. We are dressed, head to toe in Tyvek suits, heavy-duty latex gloves, shoe covers and masks to complete the ensemble. We look like two deranged Oompa Loompas from Willy Wonka's Chocolate factory. But we weren't there to make fucking chocolate.

The whole process really only takes about five minutes but it seems like forty-five minutes when we have to deal with a decomp.

We walk in with our stretcher, unzip a black body bag, and place it open side up on the stretcher. We position the stretcher in such a way that if we pull him by the legs the body will slide onto the bag and then all we have to do is zip up the bag, strap the whole thing to the stretcher and get out the door. We are breathing through our mouths to limit the smell; we are knocking the maggots off of the face of the deceased as best we can and we are swatting at the accumulating flies. We are briefly interrupted from our task at hand by a young girl in a sheriff's uniform with a camera.

"I need to get a few pictures of his back if you don't mind. Could you roll him?" So the medical examiner doesn't want this case, he hands it off to a local doctor to sign off but wants pictures for his scrapbook? I get it, it is procedure, just to document that the death was not suspicious in nature. We adhere to the girl's request and she snaps a few photos. I make a smart-ass comment about getting "my good side" and "should I smile in this picture." She takes me seriously and assures me that I will not be in the shot. Tough room. No laughs.

She finishes up and we do too. We get out of there after being assured that the doctor that the medical examiner had contacted will in fact sign the death certificate. We are given their name along with names of assumed next of kin. We load the body into our plain white "stalker van" and we are on the way. The air off, the windows open as we go dry-heaving happily down the road. Today, many funeral homes use a removal service. This is a third-party transport company charged with picking up decedents and transporting them to funeral homes and crematories.

In a case like a decomp, the family is usually advised toward cremation as a viewing or embalming is not really possible. Embalming is an act of preservation and that shipped has clearly sailed with this poor gentleman. Kenny will no doubt meet with the family in the later in the morning and advise them such. As I sit back in the passenger seat of the van I think, "Damn, they are not paying me enough for this shit." We did get paid extra to go on calls, usually about fifty bucks per case, but at times like this, one hundred isn't even enough.

It was always kind of sad to go on these though. Someone has died. Someone alone, living alone, no one around and no one knowing of their demise for weeks. What a lonely way to go. Putting aside all the ooziness and eew factor of a pickup up of a deceased under those circumstances, it still remains very sad to know that this person passed with no family around. Nobody, well, caring until the neighbors said, "Ya know what? I ain't seen em for some time now." Sad, an "unattended death," a lonely existence brought to an end in a lonely, lonely way.

The next day the funeral director will sit down with family. Then maybe they will start squabbling amongst each other for his personal belongings or money, if he had any. That part is even sadder. Where were they as this man gasped his last? Where were they for those three weeks that he lay dead? Now, they want a "piece of the pie." Now they want was is "theirs." So they choose the least expensive cremation and go on their way to bicker with each other over the house and belongings. The funeral director will, well, direct. Direct them to the fancy urn or maybe some keepsake jewelry to put ashes in, or maybe a big expensive obituary. The director will direct. Then Mr. Jones, like the multitude of other souls will be taken care of in accordance of all laws and regulations and then—forgotten.

It used to be that when the cremation was chosen, one of the members of the support staff team would have to transport the body to the cremation facility that was owned by another firm. But now we had our own and soon the body would be taken there. Having your own crematory meant that someone would have to perform the cremation. That is where the funeral directors came in. If Don was out of town or busy elsewhere the funeral directors would run down to the crematory, place one in for cremation, then head back to the funeral home to complete their myriad of daily tasks. They would then later go back to the crematory to complete the process and bring the ashes back. The crematory was miles from the actual funeral homes so the whole "back and forth" for the funeral directors became a bit tedious.

To offset the cost of the crematory, Don, and his wife had decided to start cremating for other funeral homes. Funeral homes that did not have their own cremation equipment, like the position that they themselves were once in. These would become outside or trade funeral homes. For a relatively low price, we would cremate for other funeral homes and all the funeral homes had to do was deliver the bodies and pick up the ashes. It became a great working relationship with other funeral homes. Also, around this time, again, sensing a growing trend in the industry, Don and Nancy opted to get into the direct disposer game.

With cremation becoming more and more popular and cost-effective for families, families were starting to do business with low-cost cremation services. It was cheap, economical and you didn't have a bunch of relatives you couldn't stand anyway peering down into a casket and saying, "oh look at Aunt Lulu, don't she look so natural…looks like she is just sleepin' so peaceful." Uhg. More and more people were turning toward cremation but didn't want to spend thousands of dollars to do it.

Enter the direct disposer. Admittedly, the term sounds like one of the guys hanging off the back of a large trash truck at 5:00 a.m. I mean, they could have given a better name for it. But essentially, a direct disposer is a direct low-cost cremation from a person licensed to "dispose" or give "cremation disposition" to a deceased. By law, there are no services or viewings. There are no fancy funeral homes. The deceased is simply picked up and for a low price, usually below seven hundred dollars, they are cremated and given back to the family.

It is a cheap, no-frills way to say goodbye. No services or viewings. Just pick up, cremate, return to the family, rinse, repeat. This was becoming big, big business and big competition for funeral homes. However, the two, by law, must remain completely separate. The funeral home had its building and its clientele; the direct disposer would be the same. Different building, different license and one not acknowledge the other. If a family came to the funeral home and they could not afford the $2000 cremation, then a "kindhearted" funeral director would mention that there was this little cremation business that did it for less. Either way, the money all came to our company.

Don and Nancy saw the economic upside to this and quick as a flash became sort of, their own competition. They would have the fancy funeral home with the embalming, services and viewings for those who still desired that particular tradition, *and* the direct disposer business, to offer a low-cost cremation for those who wanted simplicity and low cost. So, they set out to get two pieces of the pie.

People were rapidly turning to cremation for a number of reasons. But first and foremost was cost and convenience. You can get your loved one cremated today and say about two, three or even four weeks from now, have a nice memorial service at the church of your choice. Hell, it doesn't even have to be a church. It can be a clubhouse at a local mobile home park where they lived. It can be a restaurant, a bar or it can even be at someone's house. Cremation gives you time and flexibility. With burial on the other hand, time is *not* on your side. You have a limited amount of time to embalm, cosmetize (make-up) and casket the decedent before Uncle Herschel starts to look like a dried-up catcher's mitt.

Cremation was/is the future and if you can offer a lower price for just a cremation than what the big fancy funeral homes are charging, all the better. Don and Nancy owned the big fancy funeral home, and the fact that direct disposers were taking a bite out of their business scared them to death (pun intended). They decided to start grabbing up as much business as possible, playing both sides of the equation. They started their own direct disposer business.

That's right, for one low price—I believe it was around $550— the cremation service would pick up your loved one, cremate them and hand them back to you. No services and no viewings, no bullshit. Urns and death certificates were extra. By law, there were no viewings or services permitted. And it paid off—big! Money was coming in from the big fancy funerals, cremations, outside cremations and now, they were going after those people who wanted to save a buck but still have their loved one cremated with dignity.

There were some hiccups however, like getting any business off the ground, there are going to be oopsies and learning curves. But when the cremation service started the one huge oopsie that comes to mind was the fact that they kept the phone number from one of their old, now defunct funeral homes and made it the direct disposer line. Wow did *that* cause some confusion.

You would get to a home to pick someone up and start talking about cremation and they would freak! "No, no, no, we called the Don Williams Funeral Home number…you're not with them? We don't want cremation…what is going on?" That is where we usually had to think fast, tell them that 'Don Williams was bought out by another funeral home years ago and we picked up for them *as well as* a cremation service. We would reassure them, leave and change the paperwork and call information on the way back—uhg. There were definitely some bumps, but overall, getting into the direct disposer game was a lucrative move for Don and Nancy.

CHAPTER 3

Competition (The Blame Game and Snitches)

Between the cremations for our own funeral home and the outside funeral homes that had contracted us to cremate for them, the crematory certainly had a steady flow of business. Now, the direct disposer business was up and running and things were starting to start to heat up (again, pun intended).

The two branches of the funeral home were starting to see an increase in families choosing cremation and the outside funeral homes that we had agreed to cremate for were also starting to see an uptick in the cremation desire. Don, was running the crematory and he was relying on the funeral directors to handle the direct disposer business. The funeral directors hated this! They notoriously hated direct disposers and they now really hated having to play the part of one.

It was at this inopportune moment that Don decided that he would hand things off to the funeral directors to start keeping up with the cremations at the crematory and he would do, well, other things. The funeral directors would run back and forth to the crematory and cremate *their* cases and new cases from the direct disposer business. The outside funeral homes' cases would go ignored until someone from one of *those* outside funeral homes would call and inquire after the ashes. Now with the business coming from the direct disposer *and* several funeral homes, it was becoming clear that the crematory needed to have someone full-time to run it.

Here is how cremation works, in a nutshell. Someone dies. The family chooses cremation. Let's say, they don't want a service, just cremation. The body is transported to the Crematory and placed in refrigeration. It takes anywhere from twenty-four to seventy-two hours for the death certificate to be signed by the doctor. Once signed, the state and the medical examiner check that everything is in order and if so, permission for cremation is granted. Until this time the deceased remains in refrigeration. When all approval has been given, the crematory is notified. This is usually done by providing a permit for cremation and a form signed by the next of kin saying that they also approve cremation. In the region that I worked in, we did not even think of proceeding with cremation until:

- The permit was provided with medical examiner approval
- The family had signed a cremation authorization form
- Forty-eight hours had passed since time of death

Once all three of those had a check mark by them, it was time to cremate. Now, the cremator or "retort" is a large oven-looking machine. The outside is a large metal box with gas lines and electronics going into the top of the machine. The inside is basically a big brick oven. The bricks are a special heat retaining material that can withstand temperatures in the thousands. A human body cremates at a temperature of 1650 degrees. Some States a little more, some a little less but on average, 1600 degrees. The State ordinances dictate at what temperature the cremation will take place and remain "legal."

It takes about 2 to 2.5 hours for a body to be cremated. Before placing a body into the retort, it is usually a good idea to check for a pacemaker. Pacemakers have batteries, in fact anything with a battery should be removed from the body. These will explode under high heat and will do damage to the inside of the retort. That means that I had to perform a sort of surgery on the deceased to remove and clip wires of a pacemaker (add heart surgeon to my resume—just kidding).

Once the cremation is complete all that is left is brittle bone material. Just the skeleton and that skeleton is brittle. It crumbles like feta with the slightest touch. After the cremation, the bones and whatever is left is swept from the oven, cooled and then pulverized into a fine powder. These are the ashes that the family gets back. Everybody is identified, double-checked and tagged. There is usually a stainless-steel disc that accompanies all bodies as a further means of identification. So, are you getting back *your* loved one? If it went through my care? You bet your ass! I took every precaution and care to ensure that I was cremating the person whom I was supposed to.

Some years back cremation obtained a very bad reputation as there were some funeral homes that were found guilty of "not doing what they said they would do." We have heard the horror stories of how bodies that were supposed to be cremated were piled up in a corner and forgotten or families got back ashes and they turned out *not* to be *their* loved one or a body was mishandled or misidentified and so on and so on. There have indeed been some unscrupulous people in this business and some grave mistakes (again, pun—you know) have been made.

You see, with a cremation, there are no "do-overs" There is no "oops, my bad." You cannot undo a cremation. It is the ultimate ending. If a person is buried in the wrong plot, if they are placed in the wrong casket, have the wrong clothing placed on them or whatever, these things can all be corrected. But you cannot unburn someone.

There are mistakes and there is carelessness in this business and I saw my share of it as well. But when I was the one doing the cremation, I checked, double-checked, triple-checked and documented everything.

The crematory was several miles away from the funeral homes and for the longest time, anyone going out there to cremate was usually in a rush (big mistake). They had to get in, do what they needed to do and get out. This is where mistakes would be made. Paperwork was misfiled, ashes were "misplaced" and just an overall carelessness existed. Don and Nancy had made one or two people "in charge of cremation" but still expected those people to perform other duties during at the funeral home during the day.

For instance, they would have one of the support staff trained at the crematory and say to them, "OK, you have to cremate now. But you also have to clean the funeral homes, go pick up bodies, work services and everything else." Essentially nobody was given the job full-time. So, mistakes would be made. Nothing catastrophic, just a lot of disorganization and lost paperwork. Thankfully, I never heard of our facility cremating the wrong body or some huge mistake like that, but it has happened at other crematories around the country. It can happen and does happen. Actually, it is pretty simple to see how it can. There are a lot of t's to cross and i's to dot before the flame ever hits the body and if you are in a hurry or have a ton of other things to contend with, you are going to fuck up. Guaranteed!

The crematory facility itself, soon became a disaster area. Funeral directors or whatever staff member was saddled with cremating was spending on average, about 30 or 40 minutes at the facility, tops. They were in and out. So, things were just thrown around, paper work was piled up and there were times you could barely walk through the facility. But as long as the funeral home and the direct disposer business was making the money, who cared?

Families were waiting, on average, about two or three weeks to get the ashes of their loved-one returned to them. The outside funeral homes weren't picking up or paying for their cremations, so their ashes sat around for a month or more. Bodies were dropped off at the crematory and whenever someone had time, they would eventually be cremated. Not a real good plan of action. Especially when people had memorial services planned or the wanted to leave town with the ashes. Cremation was becoming a numbers game just like the rest of the funeral industry. Get 'em in, get 'em out and get the money. But with the outside funeral homes and direct disposer business, the crematory was now a very busy entity of this funeral establishment. It was becoming increasingly evident that they needed someone there full-time.

Meanwhile, I was working services, cleaning the funeral homes and working on call some nights. I hated it. I admit I was no longer a team player and was about to leave after spending four years in the business. I had had it. I was working eight or ten hours a day in the blistering sun lifting bodies, moving caskets, picking up dead bodies from hospitals, the medical examiner or wherever, and running to the airport to ship one out or to pick one up from a flight from up North. Then, at the end of the day, when I would be ready to kick back and relax, I would get a call to continue my day. I would have to be ready to get dressed in a suit and tie and go out to pick someone up. It could be midnight, two, three, or four in the morning. It didn't matter. The job was getting to me without a doubt.

I was also becoming disenchanted by the incompetence I was witnessing on a daily basis. Some of this was enough to make me run for the hills. Like the time we were entrusted with the care of a Jewish decedent. The casket company had sent us a Jewish Casket. This is a casket that has *no* metal or synthetic parts. It is a plain wooden box with a hinge-less lift-off lid. There is straw for the bedding and the whole thing is carried with dignity and decorum with tradition steeped in Judaism. The casket was delivered and the first thing that one of our esteemed support staff does is to open the lid. Thinking there are hinges on the lid like a regular casket and clearly not knowing anything about custom and tradition of the those they were entrusted to serve; the support staff pushed the lid upward and completely off the body of the casket. The lid hit the ground with a crashing thud and became cracked and damaged.

Then there were the times that families had food set out in the back lounge area of the funeral home for after the service. There were cookies, cake, shrimp cocktail, finger sandwiches and various soft drinks. However, when the family gathered for their luncheon, many of the shrimp, cookies and sandwiches were gone. Eaten by one of the support staff while the family was in the chapel, mourning.

Behind the scenes, if it could go wrong, it did. Miscommunication was a major problem. The funeral directors felt that if the family asked for something to be done, it wasn't necessary to share that with the staff on service day. There were never enough memorial pamphlets printed. Cars would be lined up incorrectly or the funeral home vehicles were filthy; areas of the funeral home, that everyone thought would not be used that day would have to be hurriedly cleaned and readied at the last minute because the family wanted that particular room—but again, the funeral director did not see that as an important detail.

There was a very successful local business owner whom had passed away. He was a pillar of the community and for a brief time, my wife had worked for him years earlier. His son, whom I knew, was lost. He was, however, happy to see a familiar face (mine) at the funeral home and had sort of leaned on me to make sure some things took place during the service. He even approached me during the four-hour visitation that I was working the night before. But in the eyes of my bosses, I was a peon. It was resented that I had anything to do with the family. I was not a funeral director and the funeral director in charge of the service that day, whisked me out into the parking lot at the church instead of me being "inside with the funeral service" and making sure that the family request was adhered to.

Instead, the funeral director, Joe, decided to have one of his "buddies," who didn't even work for the funeral home, be his "right hand man" that day. Oh yeah, that made sense. There, at the church, sat Don and Nancy and there was Joe and some unknown putz standing at the front of the church. Wow! It looked bad—really bad. Joe was oblivious and stupidly had no idea that this was not an opportune time to play favorites with his friends. I later learned that the son of the owner was asking after me and wanting me to help carry out his request. But again, who was I? I was just the peon out in the ninety-degree heat parking cars.

There was another time that there was an interment of ashes for one particular service. This family was personal friends of the owner, and he was going to work the services as the funeral director. Only one problem. *He* forgot the ashes. I was elected to be the one to rush them out to the cemetery. I grabbed up the urn and headed out to the cemetery. Traffic was a nightmare, I got behind a geezer doing thirty miles an hour, all the while, Don was calling me on my personal cell phone berating me and yelling at me to "get my ass out there with those ashes now! The family is waiting!" In the funeral game, the funeral director or the owner of the funeral home is the last to take the blame for anything. Something goes wrong, let's blame the low man on the ladder. Let's blame the peon support staff. That's what happened here.

When I got to the cemetery, the entire family looked in my direction as I got out of the van. They *all* looked at me as if I had just pissed on their loved one's ashes. It was clear that Don, who had screwed this up to begin with, had bashed me to the family. Don was their buddy. Don told them I was to blame. So, upon my arrival, it was very clear that I was as popular as a whore in church. The whole family glared at me. There were even some comments made about me that I keenly overheard.

This service, that day, was planned a bit backward. They were to inter the ashes and then go to the church for a service. After Don snatched the urn from me, I then was to go to the church and set things up there. There I was, professionally greeting people as they walked in. I was handing out the memorial pamphlets and when Don walked in, he came over to me and, making sure the family was in earshot, said to me, "You can go!" I returned to the funeral home, hung the keys to the van up and walked out. I had another hour left to work but oh well, I was done with the shit for the day. I was over it and wasn't really sure if I would be back. Unprofessionalism and stupidity were becoming commonplace and today I was the fall-guy. I was the one to be made to look incompetent.

The bottom line comes down to money. People like Kenny and Don, that is what they really cared about. The money. Old families with a bob or two, big land owners and police officers killed in the line were the cash cows. Twelve-, fifteen-, seventeen-thousand-dollar funerals were what the funeral directors wanted. Rich? Come see us. We will give you a great service and you'll pay for it. Poor? Well, I guess we will help if we must. And if something goes wrong, it's someone else's fault. Not the esteemed funeral directors. The funeral homes were making so much money it was unreal. The funerals, burials, cremations, outside cremations and the Direct Disposer business were all bringing in truckloads of cash. It was clear to see what/who was important.

The two branches of the funeral homes were owned by Don and Nancy. They were the same company. But two places doing the same business were never more different. It seemed as though they were in direct competition with one another. At one location, where Kenny was in charge, the support staff was to "work the parking lot" during services. Full suit and tie no matter what the weather. One hundred and five degrees? You want to stand out in the parking lot without your suit jacket? Think again! The answer was *no*! Basically, you'd be lining cars up and telling people where to park for the procession out to the cemetery. The other location, on the other hand, saw no need in this. They felt it was an outdated practice and people knew where and how to park. They felt there was no need to police the parking lot.

When it came time to spend some money, one branch got all the new stuff. Need a vehicle? It would go to branch A. Need a new pulpit, a new sound system, new lighting? Branch A.

Branch B, overseen by Carl, got the leftovers or had to make due. In fact, they had an old 1995 hearse that was in so much disrepair that the AC didn't even work in it. But was it fixed? Nope, that would be too much money. I'll never forget, it was ninety-six degrees, we had just finished a service at a church and I was to drive that piece of shit hearse. There I was with no AC, in a suit and tie, trying to look professional and sweating like a guilty witness on a courtroom stand. When I pulled up at the grave side, I didn't step out of the hearse as so much as I oozed out of it into a puddle on the ground. It was ridiculous. It stayed that way too until Don had to drive it one day. Then he felt the need to get it fixed—big surprise.

Branch A always criticized the way Branch B did things and vice-versa. They couldn't stand each other and were always comparing the number of "calls" each one had. Call it pettiness or jealousy, what have you, they honestly hated each other. I worked at both branches and saw it from both sides.

It was actually funny—when I worked at Branch A. Branch B really didn't much like me and took every opportunity to throw me under the bus. When I worked at Branch B, it was the same in reverse. Carl, I would soon learn, was as two-faced as they came. He was an extremely unhappy individual, for all his talent and skill, for all his demeanor with families. If you worked with Carl, he would joke with you and be a friend. Then, if there was something you did or if you called bullshit on something, he would trash you until the end of time and even go as far as to tattle on you to the owners. He would yell at you in front of families as I once witnessed first-hand. He was meeting with a family in *my* office at the crematory and I had the audacity to come in to grab a fax off the machine. This was not an imagined slight, or blown out of proportion by my own imagination. This was full-on. He stopped what he was talking about with the family, turned around and said, "Do you mind? You wanna get the hell out of here?" Anything to make you look small and him look big. He did it with several people as I recall. Belittling people and trash-talking them behind their back were where Carl's true talent lay.

As a recap, you had Kenny and Joe, the racist homophobes and then you had Carl, the two-faced backstabber. I honestly couldn't say which was worse, depending on the scenario. Then there was Ronald.

Ronald was another one who couldn't communicate to save his life. He was in advanced years and was close to retirement when we worked together. Ronald was not above making life hell for the support staff as well. I remember in particular the day a lady charged at me at the cemetery, because Ronald had forgotten to arrange for the grave to be set up. This family had actually had so many problems with Ronald and this instance was the icing on the shit cake.

After a service, it was up to the support staff to load the flowers and head out to the cemetery. We would then set the flowers up by the graveside and arrange everything nicely under a big tent. You had just a few minutes to do this as the key was to have everything looking good when the procession arrived. I pulled in and immediately noticed there were no chairs. There was no tent. Just a hole in the ground. That was it. What had happened was unclear but I intended to find out. I got out of the van and started to speak with the grave guys. Unbeknownst to me, one of the family members had followed me out to the grave.

Because she had constantly had communication problems with Ronald, she decided to make sure the final stage of the service would go off without a hitch. She saw what I saw. As I approached the gravediggers and started to inquire about the grave, this lady came barreling from her car and headed straight for me. She started screaming at me as if I were to blame. I apologized and turned the whole thing back onto Ronald but she wouldn't hear it. She continued to berate me. Again, the peon is catching the brunt. Me and the grave guys quickly set up chairs and did what is known as a "false set up." Just chairs and a lowering device, no tent. By the time the procession pulled up, we had enough of a set up to continue the service at the grave.

Ronald showed up and I asked, "did you forget something?" His response? "Oh, shit," he said, "I forgot to change the time with the grave people. We had it for two and the family changed it to twelve…oh, I forgot to call grave people."

Again, I got the brunt of the families' wrath. The family would eventually be discounted for that screwup and vowed to never darken the funeral home's door again.

Ronald was elderly, forgetful and not without some health issues. He was diabetic and had to keep tabs on his sugar and food intake. He cared for his ailing wife, her mother who was closing in on one-hundred and his daughter and her family. Ronald had a lot on his proverbial plate. I don't fault the man for "missing the boat" on a few cases but when anger-filled shit-storms were heaped upon Carl's branch of the funeral home, it was usually due to Ronald and his oopsies.

Then there was the time that Ronald fell into an open grave. Yes, I said he fell into an open grave. It was a hot summer day and there was a huge Hispanic service planned. A young man had tragically lost his life and the funeral home was entrusted with his care. Ronald was busy all that morning preparing for the service with his "trainee," Mark. Mark and Ronald had spent the better part of the early afternoon working this funeral service. After about two hours, it was time to go to the grave. Now, cemeteries in the south are stifling hot in the summer. Add to that the whole suit and tie thing and by the end of the day, you are wishing for your own death.

Ronald had been busy that morning and the service took place about twelve thirty. When the service came to an end and it was time to go to the grave, it was close to 3:00. The sun was absolutely brutal and Ronald had not eaten that day. A graveside portion of the services was usually, pretty straight-forward. The priest or officiant would say a few words, there would be a prayer and then the committal of the casket to the grave. The families usually were not around for the actually lowering of the casket, but in Hispanic services, the family stayed and got involved, even down to filling in the grave with dirt. There are usually Mariachi musicians and the family takes a lot of pride in seeing their loved one off. They take pride in this as this is their duty, an honor-filled task.

Again, Ronald had not eaten that day and his blood sugar was tanking. The family gave him the sign that they were ready to lower the casket and fill in the grave. Ronald then gave the grave workers the go-ahead to start taking down the tent and removing the folding chairs. At this point it was not unusual for the funeral home staff to help with this. I myself have assisted in striking many tents and folding up chairs. But on this particular day, Ronald had started to reach above his head to loosen the tent rigging. His blood sugar took a nose dive and then so did Ronald, head-first, right into the grave. People who were there described it as a house of cards falling forward. One minute, Ronald his at the foot of the open grave, the next he was face down, on top of the casket that had just been lowered. The scene was both macabre and humorous. A casket, a batch of thorny roses, carnations, lilies and then an elderly undertaker face down on top of the whole thing.

The family, sprang into action. Several of the young men at the service dove into the grave, lifted Ronald out and sat him down in a chair and started to ply him with water. He was OK, and the family could not have been more caring and nicer about their loved one not being the only occupant of the grave for a few minutes.

Just for the record, I was not a witness to this scene myself. The story was told and retold in the annals of funeral home lore. I was working at the other branch that day and when I was told what had happened—I am not proud of this—but I laughed. I laughed my ever-loving ass off. I had to catch my breath to ask if he was OK. When I was assured that he was, I laughed even harder. I mean, I am not completely heartless. It was one of the funnier moments that took place and I am pretty sure that this story is still floating around to this day.

The point here is, that shit happens. Every business has those "oopsies" that will happen from time to time. But it is how they are handled that makes all the difference in the world. Mistakes are made. Things are going to go wrong. Human error will happen and in the case of Ronald passing out into an open grave, the unforeseen can occur. But the organization that I worked for found it really easy to let their funeral directors simply blame "others" for mistakes. Many times, it was the support staff. Those who weren't paid as much, those people who "wouldn't raise a fuss and simply take it because they needed the job." These people, myself included, would get tagged with the blame. So, my laughter that day was not so much at Ronald's expense or the fact that a man who was ill suffered a humiliating fate. It came from a place of, "oh wow, let's see how they place the blame on this one!" I was growing weary of the blame game, the miscommunication and the obsessive dollars and cents mindset of "caring" for people. Shit rolls downhill and the blame-game occurred on a daily basis.

Let's be honest, that thirty-five-dollar steak you just ordered may come out bloody rare, when you ordered medium. That suit you just had tailored may have the cuffs going up past your ankle. These are mistakes, they are errors that need correction. I am not one to blame the waitress for the steak and I am not one to blame the salesperson for the ill-fitting suit. I am one to say, "hey, can we try this again?" Shit happens. In the case of someone's funeral, the family has suffered enough. There are tears and there is sadness. Emotions are raw. People want perfection, they deserve perfection. Hopefully, and in all honesty, more often than not, mistakes take place behind the scenes. But when a visible and very evident mistake occurs, no matter the business, an apology and offer to make right is called for. Period.

Those who complained to the funeral home that things did not "go as planned" were seldom apologized to. Instead, blame was placed, excuses given and then perhaps a partial refund. But more often than not, the funeral home was right and the family was just being "unreasonable." The blame game was getting really old.

Very seldom did the funeral director take any of the blame. It was usually, "oh, it was the staff, it was the cosmetic person, the embalmer" (even though the funeral director *was* the embalmer). It was always someone else. Support staff at this funeral home, "never did anything right" to hear the directors talk. We were just the shovel guys in the elephant act.

Later on, I will illustrate how this shit-storm would come down on the crematory staff and how things would be blamed on those who tried to perform a timely cremation only to be undercut and thrown under the proverbial bus needlessly. Call me crazy, but

I believe that if you make a mistake, it is honestly, *your* mistake, say so. Own up to it. That's it. No matter what business you're in. Whether your business is steaks, suits or funerals. Admit the wrong, make right, move on. Too many I saw in the funeral business didn't know how to do this.

Kenny for instance is the biggest "finger-pointer" in the biz. He is all about "playing by the rules" unless the rules apply to him. If there was a funeral home or mostly, a direct disposer business, who was doing something "shady" in his purview, he was the first one to rat them out to the State. Never-mind that he and other staff had done some less-than-ethical shit. It was always "they did this; they're doing that." Never mind the fact that he himself was as shady as they came. For instance, when phone books were a thing and phone listings, if a direct disposer business was listed under "Funeral Homes," Kenny was on the phone to the state to claim that the Direct Disposer was touting themselves as Licensed Funeral Homes, when they were *not*!

But then here is a guy, whom I witnessed on his way to picking up a deceased early one morning, viewing the houses in the neighborhood and figuring what the mortgage must be on one of these residences and then he started doing the math in his head about how much he could get off the contract. To Kenny it was all about the money. He made good money after all. He sold preneed, headstones and he could talk that family into that beautiful cherry wood casket. In his mind, he was the best funeral director out there. In his mind, he was above reproach and without fault. He was also a snitch!

The employees of the State Financial Department in Charge of Funeral Homes and Cemeteries knew Kenny by name. He was the guy to *always* snitching on other establishments about something that he viewed as hinky. Mostly it was against direct disposer businesses that he felt weren't playing by the rules. Sometimes the state would follow-up, sometimes they wouldn't, which would only prompt a follow-up call to them from Kenny. The funeral trade is a competitive one, and Kenny, whenever possible, would point his finger and drop-dime on anyone whom he felt was not playing fair. He was little more than a schoolyard bully and snitch.

Five years had passed since I got into this funeral game and I started looking toward other avenues. I was tired of taking blame for a funeral director's miscommunications. Tired of the sadness of the profession, and really tired of the late-night calls and removals. I was done. But the fact remained that the crematory was falling behind daily and things on the cremation side of the spectrum had become an unholy mess.

That is when Nancy approached me. She recognized the fact that not only was I hard-working and organized (she felt I was pedantic and had OCD) but that I would be the perfect one to run the crematory. Business in the direct disposer company was booming. The outside trade funeral homes they were cremating for had just seen their sixth funeral home to request our services. Cremations were not being performed as timely as they should be. The refrigeration at the funeral homes and the crematory were at capacity and they needed someone to take the reins. I agreed, but I had my conditions. I would run the crematory but I needed to run the crematory, not cremate one and then go get a body, not cremate one and then go back to the funeral home to mop the floor or work a service. I needed to oversee the facility. She concurred. I was now to be the Crematory Operator for two funeral homes, six outside facilities and an ever-growing Direct Disposer business. Let the games begin.

CHAPTER 4

Cremation:
From the Fat into the Fire

My placement as Crematory Operator was met with mixed feelings. The funeral directors were both relieved and resentful. It was fucking weird. They were glad that now they were going to be able to get the ashes back to the families in a timely manner. They were glad that they no longer had to drive out to the crematory, cremate, and head back to do what they needed to do at the funeral home. But they also resented the fact that I was going to have a say. After all, I was not licensed. I had gotten training on the cremator, but I was still a lowly peon who could be pushed around and talked down to. In their minds, because they knew nothing of what it took to run the crematory, all I did was put a body in the oven, turn it on and then I would sit on my ass with my feet up all day. Nothing was or could be further from the truth.

When I was given the position as crematory operator, I found that there were some things that needed to be taken care of if I was going to be successful and the crematory was going to run efficiently. The first order of business, was to clean the joint! The place was a disaster area. There were box lids, casket lids, papers and trash everywhere. The biohazard container was overflowing, paperwork and files had not been put away for over a year. Don't even get me started on the bathroom. The whole cremation facility was an unorganized mess. I had my work cut out for me. Then there were the outside funeral homes. Some had paid; some had not. Some had left bodies there to rot. This really needed to be sorted out and if the funeral homes that we dealt with bounced a check or a credit card payment hadn't gone through, it became my job to track them down and get that payment.

A sidenote on the outside funeral homes we cremated for. Many of them were simply funeral homes that did not have their own equipment. However, some were what I call "storefront establishments." This is how those work. There is a licensed funeral director. Maybe he or she is retired, or maybe they are still in the trade; either way, they keep their license up and go into a side business with another firm, inasmuch as they hang their license in another funeral home and become the director of license. This way the storefront has mostly unlicensed staff running the show, but for the big things like embalming and interments, they call on the full-fledged director to oversee that end of things. There are many small businesses that operate this way.

In fact, we cremated for a couple of these storefronts. One in particular ran a funeral establishment in one part of the state but did cremation business everywhere! They contracted crematories all over the state as "care centers" to handle their cremations, thus making them sort of a statewide chain. It was easy money for the contracted crematories. All they had to do was light the fire. It worked like this.

A removal team would pick up and deliver the body and the crematory would cremate once they got the paperwork from the storefront. There was a caveat however: you had to make it seem like you worked for this company. I found that out the hard way. I had labels on sets of ashes, or cremains. These labels would have the deceased names, cremation numbers and the name and address of our crematory. All hell broke loose one day when the owner of this one particular storefront saw our label. They called Nancy and demanded for us to do special labels for them. Essentially, by simply making a label depicting *our* name and address, I had exposed the wizard, pulled back the curtain, and shed light on the fact that the storefront was contracting their work out. They seemingly wanted to keep that little factoid under wraps. They paid on time and very little was required of us so Nancy concurred.

There was a lot of responsibility to running the crematory. Setting human bodies ablaze was only part of the job. There were supplies to order, repairs to keep up with, parts to replace when something warranted replacing and state inspections to adhere to. The phone was always ringing for the direct disposer company, and recycling needed to be shipped out, and then there would be a whole slew of bodies delivered from other funeral homes. There was this notion that since I was essentially unsupervised, I sat back and napped all day. I suppose it was elves coming in at night and cremating for everyone—Idiots.

Then there was the fact that we would have mourning families come to the crematory. Hindu and Buddhist families wanted to see. They wanted to witness their loved one going into the unit. It is their culture, it is how they said goodbye, but with the way that facility looked, that particular service had not been offered for quite some time. Now, not only did I have to clean and organize the crematory so that it ran more efficiently, I had to clean and organize it so that people coming into the place, didn't turn tail and run.

On average, I started cremating about four to five bodies a day. The funeral directors would call every once in a while, and tell me to jump and I had to ask "How high?" Many times, there would be cases that fell through the cracks, contracts and cremations which were forgotten about, and then they would send me the paperwork and beg, pretty please, to "rush that one through." Then there were the ashes. One of the things I had to "straighten out" when I got to the crematory was the fact that there was really no hard-and-fast rule about the transport and signing out of cremated remains. After-all, the funeral staff that was cremating was doing ten other things at any given time and just couldn't be bothered with anything like protocol or procedure. So I put in place some rules and some safeguards to make sure that when cremains were picked up, I knew where they were going. I kept a detailed record. I soon became very well-versed at covering my ass. My colleagues called it "being anal" or "OCD." I called it saving our license.

The heat was something else I had to contend with. The crematory stayed at a balmy 120 degrees in the summer months and bout 80 or 90 during the cooler times of the year. It was dusty, smokey, hot and sweaty all the time. There were days I would start my day at 6 AM and not get out until 6 or 7 at night, depending on the caseload. Things like larger, obese cases always put me a bit behind.

America has an obesity problem. I am part of it. I could stand to lose some pounds myself, but have you ever wondered, if a man who is 400 lbs. dies, how does one cremate him? Here is how.

When there is an obese case, and I say this with all respect to the deceased, the person is usually three-hundred-plus pounds. There are a few things that must be done. Firstly, everyone who is cremated is placed in a carboard container. This cardboard-type casket is in accordance with state laws. The deceased must be placed in a container suitable for cremation. This can be a casket made of wood but usually it is a cardboard box. At times, the person is very large and will not fit into a box. Therefore, a wooden tray must be utilized. This tray offers the support needed for such a person. The trays usually are byproducts of airport ship-ins and we will keep several on hand for larger cases.

Secondly, a large person, on the day of their cremation, must be done in the morning. The machine must be cooled down to a reasonable temperature or else the risk of fire or injury can occur. Finally, the person must be placed in headfirst. Everyone who is cremated is placed into the oven feetfirst unless they are obese. Those who weigh three hundred pounds or more must be placed into the unit headfirst. If not, you run the risk of oils and liquids emanating from the machine and catching fire. If you have ever heard on of those stories about a crematory catching fire, nine times out of ten here is what happened.

It is late in the day, two or three in the afternoon. A funeral director has promised a family that they would have the ashes of their obese loved one by the end of the day. The funeral director then puts pressure on the crematory personnel to rush the cremation through. Against their better judgement, the operator places the deceased into the already hot unit and perhaps in a rush, places them in feetfirst. Oil, fat, bodily fluids combust, and start to ooze out of the door of the retort. Then a spark or someone panicking and opening the door causes the body fat that has oozed out to catch fire. This then becomes a fire on the *outside* of the unit and before you know it, the facility is up in flames. Not good. In a case like this, someone, not knowing the extent of the damage they can do is operating a crematory and the outcome is simply disastrous. Or maybe the crematory does not catch fire but you have an abundance of black smoke emanating from the stack, alarming residents nearby and calling the fire department. When this happens, there is a very good chance of the state and EPA getting involved which could spell big fines and possibly a license revocation.

There have actually been crematories and funeral homes shut down and heavily fined for this type of scenario. Either way, the operator must be mindful and know what they are doing. In other words, it didn't matter what kind of pressure I was under form a funeral director, my answer was no if it was going to put me, the facility, or our license in jeopardy. My no was not a popular thing with the funeral directors. After all, I was still a peon in their eyes. Ask a funeral director who is in charge of their crematory and they will point to themselves or another licensed staff. Ask the operator who is in charge and they will tell you something very different.

The pecking order at a funeral establishment is ever wavering and funeral directors will feel that their word is final. Not so when it comes to the crematory. This is a very hard pill for licensed staff to swallow. It works like this. When they need me to rush one through and I do, I am their friend, though they are slow to thank me or even speak civil to me. When I cannot because my workload is backed up or for whatever reason, then I am "disagreeable and difficult to work with." Essentially, I was always only good when I kissed their asses.

Along with all of that, there was always something else to do at the crematory. If I had any "downtime," it was short-lived. There were minor repairs, supplies to be ordered, recycling of metals and dental materials that had to be sent to refineries, there were payments to take, family witness cremations and tours. Yes, I said tours.

I had an open-door policy when I ran the crematory. If a family wanted to look at the facility, I would take them on a guided tour. I charged fifty-cents per tour (just kidding). That is why it was always important that the building was kept up and things were organized. I would lead people through and explain the process. I would show them around but never ever would let them see anyone going through the cremation process or inside the refrigeration. My feeling was, that those were someone's loved one. That person in our care, was someone's uncle, aunt, brother, son, sister or daughter. That was somebody and their privacy was paramount. I would show people a very vague overall picture of what took place and how. Sometimes families just wanted to know and I was always willing to give a tour or answer any and all questions for them. It put people at ease. But again, in the minds of the funeral home staff, all I did was put a body in and take naps all day. Can you say that I put up with just a little resentment and hostility? Oh, it gets better.

CHAPTER 5

Heat, Both Literal and Figurative

I was to be trained at the crematory on the large cremation retort. All the dos and don'ts were heaped upon me as I readied myself to take the helm and get things back on track. I had spent a whole weekend, just cleaning the place. The people who were cremating there, as mentioned previously, were always in a rush and anything that could speed up the process was taken into account. If there was a casket, the lid came off; if there was a larger person, the cardboard box was put in without a lid. Linings of caskets were discarded—anywhere and rubber gloves, bio-hazardous materials, were thrown about instead of being placed in a bin. The bin was packed to the rafters, and no one had seen after it for some time anyway, but still, I don't think the floor was the right place for biohazardous materials either. The place was a mess. There were file folders stacked up and placed everywhere. Dust (ash) accumulated on everything and the office, which also, housed the office of the direct disposer was in shambles.

After my training, I started on the backlog of cases that needed to be done immediately. The first few days at the crematory were touch and go. Boxes holding deceased persons, were soggy from being in refrigeration so long, there were ashes belonging to outside funeral homes that needed to be picked up and the file drawer that held all the reports for the state was in quite a state. As I went through the cases needing to be cremated, I started to sort out the mess that was left behind. A typical day was, get the machine fired up, bring it up to temperature, get the first case of the day going and then start to go over paperwork and files that needed to be put away. It was also my job to assist with removals or funeral services. I balked at this many times as to do so meant leaving the crematory and putting me behind. That is how they got into this mess in the first place. Because I felt that my job was now to take care of cremations and the crematory, I was instantly viewed as not a team player. I was again, "the outsider."

I was tasked with cremating, filing, printing paperwork for all cremations, collecting payments from the outside funeral homes, taking care of any and all repairs to the equipment, ordering supplies, and shipping recycle materials to metal refining companies. Not to mention answering the phone and taking death calls for the direct disposer company. In short, I was entrusted to work on my own, by myself, without the watchful eye of funeral directors and administration. Nancy had trusted me. She had put me in charge of the crematory. Period.

I soon found the thick air of resentment ever-growing. No longer was I just the peon being ordered around and mopping bathrooms and scraping blood off of prep tables in the embalming room. I now had my own domain. I was the crematory operator and it pissed the funeral directors right the fuck off. I continued to have respect for those I worked for and with though it was difficult at times. If I asked for assistance, it was given but with attitude. If I needed to take a lunch, I was to still answer the phones. If I took time off, it was an opportunity for a funeral director (Carl) to come down to the crematory and scrutinize everything and surmise that everything I was doing was wrong in his eyes.

Many days I couldn't take a lunch or even get a break. There were deliveries of bodies from other funeral homes, there were walk-ins from families in need of cremation through the direct disposer company, and then there was an onslaught of bodies to be cremated or bodies in refrigeration that had been there for several weeks, and I needed to track down just what the hell was going on with them. If I called a funeral director to ask about a particular case, I was met with a, "just who the hell do you think *you* are" attitude. Thinking back, I believe just putting up with the bullshit and scratchy person-alities was more tiring than the work itself.

Then there was the heat. As I have mentioned, the cremator performed its task at a whopping 1,650 degrees Fahrenheit. This meant that the back area of the facility stayed in the hundreds of degrees almost constantly. It did not pay to air condition the back area of the facility as doing so would only trash whatever AC unit they put in in a matter of weeks. There was a big loading bay door that we kept open and that is where deliveries came in. There were a number of funeral homes that would simply show up unannounced to drop off a body for cremation. Getting a few minutes to myself seemed impossible, to say nothing of taking an hour for lunch. I recall once taking a lunch and going across town only to be called by the office manager of the funeral home asking just where the hell I was? I told her I was at lunch, she then proceeded to tell me that one of the funeral homes had shown up and was waiting for me at the crematory and I was to get back there immediately—I cancelled lunch. This caused even more shit.

Every other Friday, we were to fax our time cards to the office at Carl's funeral home. This is where Nancy's office was located and she did payroll. Carl loved this day. Not for the obvious reason of "can't wait till payday," rather, it became tattle on A. L. Day. He would grab my time card from the fax machine and run whining and crying to the owner of how I was not taking lunch and how I had overtime and how I was "robbing them," et cetera. Nancy would then come down to the crematory and give me a dressing down and ask me why this was. The resentment was almost laughable. They wanted someone to do the cremations for their families but they didn't want me. It became very evident that I was still the peon or simply just someone they didn't like.

Again, Carl was always friendly and pleasant to my face but then would throw me under the bus at every turn. It was ridiculous. The crematory was making so much money that the owners were shitting green. We would charge an outside funeral home a couple hundred dollars to cremate someone and it didn't' really cost us that much to do it in the first place. The upkeep of the facility was quite expensive, however.

From time-to-time things like new brick work or flooring was needed for the retort. We would hire a company who specialized in this, they would come out and perform the work, and then we need-ed to perform a "bake-out" of the new refractory, or concrete furnace work. This required someone starting the temperature at a low temp and raising the temperature about fifty to 100 degrees an hour all the way to the setpoint temperature of 1,650. This whole process would take over 30 hours to complete and meant that someone (me) had to be on hand to perform this.

The very first time that this was done by me, I will never for-get. Don told me that if I needed help to reach out to any one of the funeral staff and they would assist me, that way I didn't have to stay there all day and all night performing the bake-out. "Oh, OK,"

I thought. "I will hit up the funeral directors and some of the staff and see if anyone wants to make some easy money." All you have to do is sit there and every hour, raise the temp just a bit. This is where I actually *would* sit on my ass and do very little and get paid. It was easy but tedious. Anyone entrusted with this job could simply watch a movie on the computer or whatever. I reached out to everyone and what I got back was a resounding "No!" It was very clear, that nobody was interested in assisting with this. I even offered to buy dinner or lunch for them. Still the answer was no. But not just no. It was "What, are you crazy? Fuck no!"

I spent thirty-four continuous hours at the crematory, making sure the bake out was done. I would perform this task several times during my tenure with the company—all alone, with no help and no one really giving a shit. Until payday that is. That is when I would be questioned as to why I was at the crematory all those hours. And round and round we go! Uhg. Carl was crying again over my timecard.

Working at the crematory was challenging, as is surely clear by now. The volume, the heat, the deliveries and the work itself. I was going deaf in one ear, my back was starting to give, and I suffered dehydration on two or three occasions. It was the most physically demanding job in the whole industry. Then there was the stupidity and sheer lack of caring from the funeral homes I worked for.

Location A. had just gotten a large thirty-person cooler installed at their location. So any bodies they had for cremation would stay over there. They really wouldn't voluntarily bring bodies to the crematory unless they were decomp and the smell was affecting their sensibilities or if they ran out of room. It seems I was always on the phone. "Can you guys bring me the body that I have paperwork for? It's time to get them cremated." Or "You guys have four sets of paperwork for bodies I don't have; would it be possible to transport those bodies over here?" I was constantly told, "You want 'em? Come get 'em yourself, we are busy with 'real funerals." Or, "we don't have the staff—can't get them over there." It actually would take a week at times to get a body brought over.

When the funeral directors needed something from me, then it was, "Oh, pretty please, can you put a rush on this one—the family is leaving town and I promised them that they would have their cremains." The funeral directors wanted what they wanted when they wanted it. But it would almost take an act of Congress for them to transport bodies to me in a timely fashion. It was a vicious cycle and an ongoing battle. I was the hero when I "rushed one through" but a zero when I had the audacity to expect something from them.

As for the finished result of the cremation—the ashes, or cremains—It was up to me to cremate but the funeral homes, including the outside funeral homes had to pick the cremated remains up in order to get them to their families they were servicing. This is where more fuckups occurred. As difficult as it was to get bodies delivered, it was almost a shit show to get the cremains picked up and into the right hands. My job was to cremate. In accordance with the laws and regulations of our state, I was to perform a cremation and release the ashes back to where they were going.

Again, miscommunication and the blame game reared their ugly heads. Every so often the funeral home would employ older people to help with services and visitations. They would become support staff, though their abilities were limited. Kenny had hired an older gentleman by the name of Henry. Henry was a preacher and a man of about seventy. He was at the funeral home one bright summer afternoon when a family came in to pick up the ashes of their loved one. Henry asked what the name of the deceased was, the family told him, and Henry toddled on into the office to retrieve the cremains. He found the ashes, had the family member sign for them, and sent them out the door on their merry way. He simply did what he thought he was supposed to do. You see, Henry was the only one in the office area of the funeral home at that moment. The other staff was either elsewhere working on something else, or out of the building all together. Nobody had instructed Henry in any way.

Later that day an extremely irate family member called the funeral home and started cussing out whoever answered the phone. Apparently, this particular family member, the next of kin, had given explicit instructions to their funeral director (Kenny) that under no circumstances should the ashes be given to anyone but her. It was not she who came to pick up the ashes. Instead, another member of the family, one whom this next of kin did *not* want to have access to the ashes, had been handed them. Henry had not known this; this was not communicated with anyone at the funeral home. Where were these instructions? They were on a Post-it note stuck to the front of the family's file and this file was underneath several other files and garbage on Kenny's desk. Kenny, in true Kenny fashion, had not relayed this information.

Lawsuits were threatened, the owners were contacted. All the while, I thought, "Is this, in anyway going to come back to me?" It was a fleeting thought as I said to myself, "Naaaah, I did my job. I cremated the person and got the ashes back to the funeral home. I am not involved in this at all." Oh, how stupid I was. How naïve. In the weeks that followed, again the blame game was played and Kenny's finger-pointing was directed at me. Kenny simply did not and would never take blame for anything. If he screwed up (and he did, believe me) he was always quick to deflect the blame onto someone else. I called it the "Kenny Scramble." He would literally rifle through his feeble mind and come up with someone else to blame. This time, "let's blame the crematory guy."

It went like this. I had been cremating about two or three years when this happened. I was still new when it came to ordering supplies and what I could and could not order. I figured my timecard was so closely scrutinized that if I placed an order for supplies, that too would be questioned. So, it never dawned on me to order professional looking labels for the cremains. I would simply write the name, the cremation number and the funeral home name on the box of ashes. Granted, my writing is not that great but it was legible. Kenny decided to hone in on this. "A.L. writes like a second-grader. This is the reason the ashes were given to the wrong person. A.L. and Henry are to blame!" No, Kenny was to blame, it was only *his* family, it was *his* noncommunication that caused this upset!

Nancy called me and started to berate me and instruct me that I was to make a whole new release form for all ashes. I was to place on that release form whom should receive the cremains. When I told Nancy that this information was not always made clear to me, she combatted that by saying, "If the funeral director doesn't give you that information, you are to call them and demand that info." Yeah, right, I couldn't even get the bodies half the time; they all hated me, now I am supposed to "demand" correct information from them. Again, the blame game had been played and I wound up on the bottom of the deck. I then ordered a shitload of labels and started to request proper information on all authorization forms signed by the family. I became even *more* popular thereafter.

I was called a "dick," an "asshole," and tattled on for "being mean." Again, in their eyes, I was nobody and certainly was not in a position of authority and how dare I demand anything from the royal funeral directors!

There was also the time that an expensive custom urn was ordered and upon receipt, promptly lost. Thank goodness the ashes had not yet gone into the urn. But then, there were those instances as well. There have been a multitude of times I was called at the crematory by a frantic office staff or funeral director wanting to know where the cremains were for a certain customer. I would then look at my aforementioned detailed records and inform them that those ashes had been picked up by one of the staff several days ago. Oh my God. Lost ashes! They lost someone's dearly departed! They would be lost. Found eventually, but lost for about an hour. Oh, silly them, they had "mislaid" them. Oops! What fact that these esteemed professionals seemed to miss was that this was somebody! They had lost a human being. In cremated form, in ashes, but still, these ashes were somebody! Again, it became commonplace for me to cover my ass and document everything.

I would also get calls from the same frantic people about bodies. "Is Mrs. Johnson in your refrigeration?"

"No," I would answer. "Who is that?"

"Oh," the voice on the other end would reply. "Um, we got a call yesterday and I thought she had been picked up from the hospital. I guess we never got her, never mind."

If you are thinking that this is some scary shit, you'd be right. If people knew what takes place behind the scenes at some funeral homes, they would most assuredly think twice about doing any business with these places.

Nine times out of ten, mistakes that were made all boiled down to miscommunication. This funeral director didn't relay this information, so this body wasn't picked up; these cremains were never placed in their urn; this paperwork was never sent to the crematory, and now the family is mad that their granny hasn't been cremated yet. I always loved that one. Again, the funeral director or funeral home staff would simply blame the crematory. I actually had one funeral director tell a family that the crematory was closed for the week. What the funeral director didn't know was that the family he told that to were personal friends of mine, so this bullshit story got back to me and I reassured them that I was not closed and I would get their loved one cremated.

It is beyond me how with all the miscommunication and mistakes, this organization had not been sued more. I was now cremating about five bodies a day on average. I was constantly busy. There would be a slow-down but not often. The funny thing is, when the funeral homes were slow, they thought I was too. Not true. I still had eight outside funeral homes I was cremating for, and the machine almost never stopped. Admittedly, I would have days where I did only one or two, but those days were few and far between. I worked by myself and was entrusted to do so. Rarely was I just sitting around. But again, to hear the talk at the funeral home, that is exactly what I was doing. Gossip and bullshit exist in every line of work and at every company. People will zone in on a person who works in another department, away from everyone else and talk shit about them and that talk is often overheard or it gets back to the targeted individual. It was clear that I had become a sort of whipping boy in this organization.

But the one constant in life is change. Personnel soon changed at the funeral homes. A little over a year after Mark had become a licensed funeral director, he moved on to greener pastures. He obtained a position at another funeral home, one that would not view him as a peon, but as a licensed professional. In his place was hired Jack. Jack would work at Branch A and he was a nice enough guy but he brought to the table a whole lot of personal issues and demons. He was good with families, though his speaking style was a little hard to understand (think, Boomhaur from *King of the Hill*) and he was very easily distracted to the point of letting many things fall through the cracks. There was support staff change as well. Billy, who was my backup at the crematory whenever I went on vacation, had had enough as well and left. They didn't see a need to replace him and they didn't see a need to tell me. Therefore, I no longer had anyone to "man the helm" if I went on vacation. What did this mean? This meant I got no vacation. If I did take any time off, I would only have to work that much harder to get caught up when I came back, so vacation actually became punishment.

Then, in an effort to gain more Hispanic business, Mary was hired. She became a funeral director at Branch B under Carl. She was bilingual and fairly new as a funeral director. She was nice enough, seemed to know her stuff and was hardworking. However, she knew *nothing* about cremation and could never seem to understand why I couldn't or wouldn't do a large case or a full-sized casket late in the day. She viewed that I was just being mean but in reality, I was simply trying *not* to burn the crematory to the ground.

A third new hire, Dara would soon come on board. Dara, worked in another field and like so many others, came to the funeral industry later in life. Kenny immediately took her under his wing and she soon became just as smarmy and as condescending as he was. She would smile in your face one minute and then snap your head off the next. She threw her "authority" around like a circus performer throwing knives. She thought, like Kenny, that she was the future of the funeral industry.

A little sidenote on Dara. She had attended classes online to get her license and was immediately hailed by Kenny as a really sharp and knowledgeable funeral director. However, when Mark, years earlier, had gotten his degree by attending the very same online university, he was laughed at and called "not a real funeral director." In Kenny's mind, the only true way to be a funeral director was to go to a brick-and-mortar mortuary college like he, Joe and Carl did. Anything less and you were shit. That is, until Dara came along. Dara, to Kenny, was the second coming of Christ and everyone was so fearful of her for some strange reason. I, having always had a talent for pissing people off, made no bones about the fact that I didn't care for her and was not intimidated like the rest. I found her snotty and demeaning and basically, told her as much. She was not a big fan of mine either.

The British bulldog administrator would also leave and be replaced by Joann. Again, nice enough person, but like everyone else, you never knew where you stood with her. She was the kind to lend a sympathetic ear and then the minute she was done talking to you, would trash you to the rest of the staff. Great! Another one with more faces than personality.

No matter the personnel changes, I stayed to myself at the crematory. I figured the fewer interactions I had with the rest of the staff, the happier I would be. The crematory was so busy I really couldn't be bothered with what anyone thought of me. I stayed busy—at least I thought I did. Then a little thing called COVID hit.

CHAPTER 6

The Plague

December 27, 2019, I was sick. Whoa, was I sick. A fever, sore throat, a cough that would not let up, so I went to a walk-in clinic. The staff there shrugged, said, "There is a bad flu going around," and gave me some antibiotics and an inhaler. They didn't help. During this time, as bad as I felt, I missed about one and a half days of work. I continued to wheeze and cough my way through the job of crematory manager. I felt like hell, but my attitude was that as bad as I was feeling, the people in my care had it worse. I seldom missed work. Even though the job was wearing on me and I was really over it with the people I worked for and with, I still knew that I had a job to do and I would always give it my all. But, man, was I sick. It took every bit of four or five weeks for me to completely rid myself of that "flu crud." But it was around that time, late January of 2020, that this coronavirus was taking a foothold in the US.

It "started" in the north-western part of the nation and then soon spread from there. I placed the word "started" in quotations because really, if we are honest, we don't know where in the US it started. We know that that north-western area was the first to report and document it, but where, how, why it started is anyone's guess. My feeling is, that was the worst flu I had ever encountered, and I am truly convinced that had a test been available at that time, I would have been positive for the virus. I am blessed and lucky,

I feel, to be alive as during the time I was sick, I was scared out of my mind and unsure of what was happening. As the news unfolded in the days, weeks and months following and we were all becoming very aware of the symptoms, it was clear that that virus could have very well been the thing that knocked me for a loop.

February, March, April passed. People were getting sick and dying from this. We had seen an uptick in the cases at the funeral homes and I became busier at the crematory. There was a lockdown then, not a lock-down. Nonessential businesses were closing shop for weeks or months and people were uncertain about the rules. "Do I wear a mask? Do I not wear a mask? Am I supposed to stay six feet away from people, can I not visit my granny at the nursing home? What can or can't I do?" Everyday there were new guidelines and rules and the whole thing soon turned, well, political. Not since 1918 had there been a vast pandemic and if there was a way for this country to fuck things up, we did. The red states were proclaiming that it was a government ploy to keep people in tow; the blue states were saying, "Hey, let's listen to science and those in the know." Kenny, Carl, Jack and Joe at the funeral homes were laughing it up and counting the money. They were not taking it seriously—at all. "It's just the flu, you're only dying if you're a fat-ass or you have a million things wrong with you." This was just one of the many ignorant comments made by Kenny.

Even for health and safety purposes and in the name of protecting the staff, any and all protocols that were put in place to keep us all safe were being vastly ignored. The owner and his wife were attempting to follow state and federal guidelines, but Kenny and Joe couldn't be bothered. Wear a mask? "No." No large services? "Nope, we will lose money." Wipe down everything on a daily basis with antibacterial spray? "Naaah, who's got time for that shit." At the crematory, I instituted protocols that were laughed at and ignored. The outside funeral homes I worked with, followed suit. They understood. However, my own coworkers and superiors laughed in my face, when they weren't coughing in it. It became this big pissing match. Dyed in the wool right-wing extremists like Kenny and Joe were ignoring all protections put in place and would call anyone who wore a mask or wish to take precautions, a "pussy."

Of course, this shit fell hard on the support staff. The fact was, that in the role of support staff, you had to go into nursing homes and hospitals and as the months rolled on, these were becoming ground zero for the spread of the virus. I was becoming more concerned. I was at the crematory and I was not doing removals but others were. I was keeping tabs on the reports in the local paper as to where the hotbeds of infection were. The news would report on nursing homes and hospitals with the highest number of cases. I then made the oh-so-grave error of sending an email to my colleagues informing them of this. It was just a simple link to the news publication and a sort of "be careful" type of thing. I was called by Nancy and slapped down for "stirring the pot."

Things were getting ugly fast. At the start of 2021, many people were dying from this virus. It was scary and was hitting the funeral homes and battle lines were drawn. There was a staff member whom did not feel safe being asked to go into a "Covid ward" of a hospital. They were fearful and trying to stay safe as more and more people were dying and being asked to go into a minefield of virus was not a comfortable situation. But working with the likes of Kenny, Carl and Joe it was becoming harder to stay safe. It was coming down to, "go into that ward or lose your job." They even got Don and Nancy to back them up. It was a scary time and if there was push-back, then it was seen as insubordination.

We were not nurses; we were not doctors and we sure as hell didn't get nurse or doctor pay! So not only were battle lines being drawn but threats were being made. More staff was getting sick and still showing up to work, thus infecting others. One director had even sat down with a family, maskless, coughed throughout the entire conference *and* she was COVID-positive. When the family she had met with learned of this, they were pissed! Still, in the eyes of Kenny, Carl, Joe and Jack, the virus was "nothing to worry about." Of course, with the irate family, Kenny took the other director's side and from there more battles raged. Under Don and Nancy, they had even offered to pay you even if you stayed home. Before, if you got sick and called out, it was taken off your vacation time. But this was serious, and Don and Nancy realized this and made certain allowances. But noooo, staying home showed that you were weak, "a pussy." We even had people keeping their illness a secret. They would test positive and tell no one. It was ridiculous and nothing short of life-threatening. It was absolute insanity. Kenny and Joe would downplay the whole thing and say it was nothing more than "a heavy flu," but there was no denying the uptick in deaths.

At the crematory, again, I was being called, "a dick" if I expected someone to wear a mask. I worked alone, so I wasn't in contact with a lot of people, but when staff came to the crematory, I simply asked them to follow protocol. Yeah, that went over well. In 2021 all hell broke loose. I was losing friends to this pandemic. I was having to cremate some of those friends. I had to cremate people I loved and was close to. When my workload started to contain familiar names and faces, it was all I could do to hold it together.

April, May, June July and August of 2021 were some of the worst months I had seen.

During this time, my day would start at four in the morning and I would not leave the crematory until seven or eight at night. I was now cremating seven to ten bodies a day simply so that we would have enough room to store the many more that were coming in. On Facebook I witnessed "friends" calling the pandemic a hoax and poo-pooing the notion of any sort of vaccination. At the crematory, I was cremating through one machine one hundred bodies a month. In July and August, normally, things were slow. It was summertime, and funeral homes in this area slowed down. Not this particular year however. It was full-blown Armageddon. The outside funeral homes I was cremating for were backed up, Hospitals had hired refrigeration trucks to act as makeshift morgues and still we had people, at our own funeral home who were simply shrugging it off. Their attitude was, if you weren't sick or obese in the first place, you had nothing to worry about. I would clear out some cooler space at the crematory only in time for them to be filled again with out-side cremations. The bodies didn't stop coming. In fact, one funeral home I dealt with had a particularly hard time as five members of the same family had all expired from the illness. They had two buri-als and the rest were cremations. No one had ever seen anything like it. I asked the funeral directors of other funeral homes. They all said the same thing. "No, we have never seen anything like this."

I was working six and seven days a week and still couldn't get caught up. There were days where I was suffering from dehydration and nausea as the heat and the workload had become too much. The floor all around the retort was littered with stretchers, makeshift ta-bles, church-trucks (those folding racks on wheels that held caskets) all with bodies on them. My goal was to clear out all the bodies that wouldn't fit in the cooler and then if I could get a couple more done, and clear out some more space, it was a good day.

Between June and September of 2021, I had done 450 bodies. By the end of the year, I had totaled 1,065 cremations. It is the highest number of cremations ever done by that crematory in the whole time it had been in operation. I had not gotten a vacation that year and the following year would be the same. I had no one to back me up and if I did take a day off, it was met with disdain. I couldn't win. By November of 2021, things had started to slow down a bit. We still had COVID deaths coming into the crematory but the numbers were decreasing.

In the meantime, just a moment too late, Don and Nancy had purchased a second cremation unit for the crematory. They had placed, for whatever reason, Kenny in charge of choosing the new machine. Now, Kenny was starting to dictate what was to take place at the crematory. He started to mandate, what recycling company I could and should use; he was mandating, what machine we were going to get and really started to "have a say" as to how the crematory was going to be run. Needless to say, we butted heads. I mean, here is a guy who has always hated cremation, was resentful toward me running the crematory and now he was calling the shots? I called bullshit!

But because Nancy knew even less about cremations and the crematory than Kenny, she entrusted him with the decision-making power on this new purchase. I had to tow the line and listen to this ass-bag now and it was becoming clear that I really had no say. I had been the crematory manager for the past eight years, had held the whole place together and had just seen the facility through a major global pandemic. I had made contacts in many crematory companies and retailers and knew what kind of machine we needed. I was the one who would be using these machines, but still they felt no need to involve me at all in the decision-making process. I would soon learn the reason behind this.

Kenny was in charge. The machine was delivered in June of 2021 right in the middle of the Pandemic shit storm and because it came missing some very essential parts, did not get up and running until November of that year. By this time, things had started to slow down on the COVID front. So, a second machine was a bit too little, too late. But, nonetheless, we finally had a much-needed second crematory retort!

The announcement was made that we now had two cremation retorts and I was going to able to finish out the year on a very strong note. Finally, this would take some of the load off and help me to stay afloat in the event of another global crisis or at least a very busy season. We were now we cremating for eleven outside funeral homes, our funeral homes and the direct disposer business, so the fact that we now have two ovens was a welcome announcement. But there was another announcement on the horizon, one that would shake me to my core and leave a very bitter taste in my mouth about this profession altogether.

CHAPTER 7

On Call

From my first night on call, I was not a fan! I had just worked a visitation that didn't end until almost ten thirty at night. I had worked a full eight-hour day and now I had to work a visitation. Visitations usually went from six to nine but that did not mean we would close the doors and turn out the lights at nine. It meant that the visitation ended whenever the family felt like leaving. We were prohibited from asking the family, to "finish up" and make their way to the door. We were further prohibited from rushing families along. If the visitation ended at eight or nine, then we would simply do subtle things, like turn off the music or a couple of lamps. But under no circumstances were we ever allowed to make any sort of announcement to the fact that the visitation had come to an end. In essence, we got to leave when the family left.

That is until one night when my friend and coworker Gary was working a visitation and all of the sudden, the power went out and the whole funeral home when dark. People screamed and freaked out immediately. I get it. The last place you want to be in the dark, without power, is a funeral home with the corpse right there in the room with you. The outage only lasted about a minute, but as soon as the lights came back on, people gathered their shit and got out of there!

My first night on call was a Friday night, the family in question had scheduled their visitation from six to nine. But come nine o' clock, they weren't budging. There were more tears and more people walking in to pay their respects. At about ten thirty, the last of the family had filed out the door. I was alone in the funeral home at last. I started to walk through the funeral home, turning off lights and locking doors. By the time I had completed my rounds and got to my car, it was eleven. I got home, took off my tie, and had successfully unbuttoned three buttons on my shirt when my cell phone rang. It was Joe, they had a "house call." This meant a decedent had passed away at home, usually under hospice care, and we had to go retrieve the body. Joe didn't like doing after-hours calls any more than the rest of us so he had suckered another support staff to meet me at the funeral home and this person and I would go pick the deceased up. Evidently, my day was not over

That was my first after hours call and I remember it as if it happened yesterday. We met at the funeral home and went on the call. The gentleman was under hospice care. He had just been transported back home earlier that afternoon. Doctors had said he had another week or two. Not true. He passed that very night. The family, particularly the wife, was destroyed. She was so overcome with grief. It was a difficult situation to walk into. Two funeral home staff would always go to houses. For nursing homes, hospitals or "institutional calls" as they were known, one person could make the removal. When it was a house, there were stairs, corners, narrow hallways to contend with and two people were better in those situations.

We performed our task with dignity and care and brought the body back to the funeral home. He was to be a cremation, so into refrigeration he went. If they were to be embalmed, the body would be placed on one of the stainless-steel tables in the prep room, stripped of all clothing or hospital gowns and await embalming. The funeral home I worked for believed—and it is a little-known fact—that the sooner the embalming takes place, the better the result. Therefore, an hour or two after arriving at the funeral home, in the case of an embalming, the funeral director who was on call, would arrive and perform the embalming. But this family had chosen cremation, so no embalming was necessary. Into the cooler he went and back home I went. Now it was close to 1:30 a.m. and I was beat. I knew I had to be up by six thirty to get into work the next morning by eight. Being on call really sucked.

After deciding that I would not become a funeral director, I chose to go back to school. I started working toward a bachelor's degree in history and wanted to go into teaching. I knew two things: I did not want to become a licensed funeral director and I needed further education in order to find other employment. I soon signed up for online classes with an accredited university. There I was, in my forties, taking classes that quite frankly I should have taken years ago. It was difficult. I was working full-time and going to school. There would be times, particularly at the end of a course where I would need to beg off being on call. This infuriated the funeral directors. Again, I was a "pussy" who didn't want to work. The fact was, I was working my ass off for the sole purpose of not having to do this job for the rest of my life. I was tattled on, again. I had more than one dressing down by my bosses as to why I was needing my evenings to myself to study and take exams. It didn't matter to them. If I wasn't 100 percent working for the funeral home around the clock, I wasn't a "team player." So be it.

I never hid my feeling that being on call was a pain in the ass. You weren't paid to be on call, so if you didn't get called, you didn't get paid. You would cancel any life or plans you may have had for the purpose of staying at home all night waiting for your damned phone to ring. Then when it did, you were expected to jump and get dressed and be at the funeral home in record time. There was one instance where one of the support staff had worked eleven hours, went home and was on call. When he was called, he had the audacity to get a shower first and then got dressed. When you went on a call it was full suit and tie. Professional and polished. If you opted not to wear your tie, it was noted and frowned upon. Anyway, this man got to the funeral home to meet the other staff who was already there and waiting on him. He was reprimanded the next day for not "being faster" about getting to the funeral home. It was crazy and often unreasonable.

Then there was protocol. There were funeral directors whom you didn't mind going on calls with and then there were those whom you dreaded. For instance, Joe was good with families but his methods were a bit old-school. He didn't believe in using latex gloves for his protection. His feeling was, if you put on gloves in front of the family, you are insulting them. He would say, "It's like you were saying that their loved one was 'germy' and it is a slap in their face." But then again, this was a guy who would perform an early morning embalming while eating an Egg McMuffin. "Germs" were not of concern to this guy. I didn't care what he said or thought, I was wearing fucking gloves. I even pointed out the fact that in some cases hospice nurses and doctors were tending to this person all while wearing gloves. Really, the family was never offended by gloves. Then again, Joe and Kenny are the same guys who said that COVID was just a bad flu and if you are healthy to begin with, it's nothing to worry about. Idiots.

Joe was also a guy who urinated on a support staff's car because they had parked in his spot. Joe was a skilled embalmer and good guy overall, but had a bolt or two coming loose. You really never knew where you stood with Joe. He would be nice one minute and then remind you he was packing a gun the next. You really had to walk quietly around him at times.

As support staff you were not to speak unless spoken to. You were never to speak to the families and you sure as hell were never supposed to have any ideas of your own. Two of the funeral directors I worked for were adamantly pissed if a family member spoke to us and we answered any of their questions. They didn't want us interacting with the family at all. In fact, if you went on a house call with Ronald, he would leave you in the car while he went in and talked to the family. Then, when it was time to transport the body from the house to the car, you would be summoned. I went along with this all the way until the day he turned off the engine and left me in a one-hundred-degree vehicle like a forgotten dog. On the next call with Ronald, when he said, "You wait here," I said, "Bullshit! I am coming in with you!" Support staff were commonly treated like second class citizens. We were not viewed as anything but bodies who moved bodies and I was tiring of it. We were expendable. But heavily relied upon. When the funeral directors were tired and didn't want to go on a call, sending two support staff to a house call was fine.

Two, three, four in the morning. That cell phone ringing was a bitter pill to swallow. I had to keep telling myself that I was doing a service for families. That was what I always had to keep in the forefront of my mind. I was helping others. Did it make it easier? No. But I knew that I had a job to do. When I was on call, my life stopped. I stayed home, stayed in my suit and tie and was ready to go at a moment's notice. But then, there would be those times where Forest Gump, Kenny's son, would "steal calls."

He would tell the funeral directors that he would take call even when I was on call. There I would be, sitting at home, waiting and he would be the one who was called. See? Nepotism has its benefits. He took four calls one night while I was the one who was supposed to be on call. At fifty dollars per call, he essentially stole two hundred dollars from me. When I came in the next morning and found that I had been cheated out of that money, I was pissed. See, a couple weeks before, I had asked not to be on call or work visitations that week as I had a challenging class coming to an end. The class and the week ended and I was placed back on call but because I couldn't be on call the week prior, I was punished. Shit like this took place all the time.

The funeral home I worked for was really the only area funeral home that still sent their own staff on calls. Other funeral homes in the area, long ago, discovered that staff worked better during the day if they weren't out at all hours during the night picking up corpses. It made sense, just not to the funeral home I worked for. They still did things "old-school" and felt it looked better if our own staff was the first face that the family saw. I get it, but when that first face that the family sees is an idiot or an overworked, tired-ass staff member, it really does little to help instill confidence.

Bottom line: being on call for a funeral home was intense and much is expected. Your life takes a back seat and you are expected to jump through hoops at all hour's day and night for a little bit of money. I have more than once gotten to a house only to be told not to take the body because a brother who lives thirty miles away is coming and wants to see the deceased before we take them. So, we wait and wait and wait. Then there are those time when a daughter or wife has climbed into bed with the deceased and is refusing to leave their side, so we can perform our task, or a loyal dog is standing between us and the bed that the deceased is occupying, growling and not willing to let us anywhere near them.

Don't get me wrong, these are all extremely heart-breaking scenarios and the grief is very real; it just makes our job that much more difficult. I have picked up decedents from mansion floors, from toilets in mobile homes and from one room shacks. I have dealt with purging leaking bodies, maggots and flies. I have held the hand of a wife as her other hand gripped that of her deceased husband of forty years. I have seen a wife fall on top of the body of her dead husband and sob uncontrollably until she is hyperventilating. I have also seen smiling spouses who have been the sole source of care for their very ill loved one and are experiencing a grief that manifests itself in relief that they are no longer in pain and suffering. I have held hands in a circle where a preacher has led us in prayer with the family. I have witnessed all the stages of grief, and I have tried to help. I have also driven away from homes, nursing homes and hospitals after going on a call I didn't want to go on in the first place a little wiser and admonishing myself for bitching about having to get up at two in the morning when these people are going through so much more.

It is about caring. Period. While never an easy part of the job, it was part of the job. As I've made it clear by now, I hated being on call, but I really believe I learned the most by going on these calls. I learned about people. I learned about their faiths and their beliefs, and I learned about my own values and that which I hold dear. Let's face it, the moment I left that house or that facility, I was forgotten and never thought of again by the family. But in that moment, I feel, I helped them in some way.

In the years to come I too would face my own crippling grief. I too would come face to face, toe to toe with that which I believed and I would simply want someone to be there for me in that moment.

As my job of running the crematory became more demanding, I no longer did after-hours calls. It was just too physically draining. I would spend all day in 120-degree heat and then have to be on call that night still with dust and ash in my hair and lungs. It was becoming too difficult and I had asked my higher-ups to cross me off the list of on-call staff. I had become older and much of that aging was due to the demands of running a crematory. They begrudgingly accepted, and I would no longer be on call at night. This brought a bit more resentment my way, of course. But there was other news on the horizon.

CHAPTER 8

Sold!

As you come into contact with funeral homes out of the necessity of burying or cremating your loved one you will find that very few of these firms are the old-fashioned family-run establishments of old. Death is big, big business and there are several large companies that have swallowed up old mom n pop funeral homes like M&M'S. SCI, which stands for Service Corporation International remains one of the largest funeral and aftercare corporations in America and around the world. They are publicly traded and chances are they own and operate a funeral home in your town that you thought was family-owned. Their MO is crafty. They make an offer and buy an old established funeral home, one that has a long-standing tradition of service in the community. They don't change the name, in fact the only thing they change is behind-the-scenes operation.

They buy, let's say, McGillicuddy's Funeral Home. Old man McGillicuddy died twenty years ago. His son and grandsons and other staff run the place. If someone dies in that town, it is usually McGillicuddy's that takes care of them. They are well established. SCI, does their research, they see this cash cow, and they make an offer to the McGillicuddy family. It's an offer they can't refuse, to use the vernacular of Vito Corleone. The family sells to SCI. SCI comes in and they clean house. They hire some, fire some and mold everything to their high-sales style of doing business. The townsfolk know nothing. As far as anyone knows the McGillicuddy family is still doing business as always. Not true. The sign in front of McGillicuddy's changes slightly. A moniker of "Dignity" is now emblazoned on the sign. If SCI owns a funeral home, they fall under the trademark of "Dignity." Now the sign out front may read, "McGillicuddy Family Funeral Home, A Dignity Funeral Home," or something along those lines. That lets all the other funeral homes in the area that they are now corporate owned by SCI. It's like a code word.

There are several "death-care" corporations out there." SCI, Keystone, StoneMor Partners, Carriage Services and Foundation Partners Group—these are just a few of the mega corporations buying up family funeral establishments all across the country and world. So that mom-and-pop funeral home that granny is laid out in is more than likely one of thousands owned and operated by big corporate America. The old-style family-run funeral home is quickly becoming a thing of the past. As is the case in many businesses nowadays, corporations are swooping in and getting a piece of this lucrative action. Let's face it, Amazon started out as a wholesale text book distributor operating out of Jeff Bezos's garage; now look at it. Just like Walmart, Apple, Google, Amazon, death and dying is also big business. From hospice companies, nursing home corporations, and right down to the makeup guy putting the finishing touches on Granny or driving the hearse, death is big money and corporations are in it to win it!

The funeral directors whom I worked for and with had all worked for corporate funeral homes in the past and all hated it. I heard the stories of hard-sell tactics and corporate pressure, stories of how if you didn't make your sales quota, you were sent to a central prep facility and told to embalm all day, and so on. Corporate call centers that took death calls and handed them off to area funeral homes. Corporations that owned funeral homes, crematories, and cemeteries everywhere like a macabre monopoly, and those old-timer funeral directors who wanted to retire selling out to these interests and riding off into the sunset. But, shhh, their names are still on the sign—no one has to know a change ever took place.

There have also been news stories of large corporations and some less than honest practices. Things like reselling cemetery plots and discarding the former occupants into densely wooded areas, preneed scams and shady contracts. Of course, those are just all hyped-up news stories (wink, google them).

The point is, even the old-time funeral home that perhaps your family has done business with for years is no longer what you think. Many have become spokes in a great big corporate wheel. Oh, sure they may keep one or two of the old McGillicuddy's on staff for appearance's sake, but that is where the "family-run" notion stops. The funeral home and staff answer to a higher calling—management teams and VPs.

It was November of 2021, when Nancy came to the crematory. She never came to the crematory. I didn't even think she knew where the hell the damned place was. Oh sure, she had been there a couple of times to chew my ass out when Carl cried about my time-card and the overtime I was getting, but for the most part, she seldom darkened my door. But on this November day, she was there to tell me that the funeral home had been sold. Foundation Partners Group (FPG) had acquired both funeral homes and crematory. This was not really a shock to me. Years earlier Don and Nancy had divorced but had remained business partners. Nancy liked the money that came from being a co-owner of the funeral home but was no longer willing to remain in the business with her ex. Don, on the other hand was not really willing to sell, but again, they were made an offer they couldn't refuse (It is not by accident that I use this Mafia phrasing here).

Nancy was tiring of the bullshit that came with running a business, she was tiring of Kenny, Joe, Dara, Carl and Mary and she was tiring of me. It seemed I was constantly at odds with the directors and staff of the funeral homes. We were butting heads more and more. I was doing my job and doing it very well, we were making a lot of money and COVID had really put a little more cha-ching into the bank. I had made a lot of money as well with the overtime and the countless hours I was putting in at the crematory, coupled with bonuses for churning out a whole lot of cremations during the whole pandemic. But FPG had noticed an uptick in funeral home biz and came to Don and Nancy with an offer. They already owned a several funeral homes in the area and Don and Nancy's establishment looked just right for the picking. Nancy came to me with this news at the beginning of November. We would become a part of FPG at the beginning of December. This was apparently a deal they had been working on for some time and now decided to tell the staff. Everyone was shocked, amazed and dismayed. The funeral directors who had toiled for corporate operations in the past were upset and angered. Well, with the exception of Kenny.

Kenny was the biggest anti-corporate squawker there was. The whole reason he came to work for Nancy and Don many years earlier was to get away from a corporate funeral home and the corporate way of doing things. But now, here it was. We were going to be under a corporate flag and Kenny was ready to wave the flag proudly after told he would get a fat promotion to "location leader" and an even fatter paycheck. Yep, you want to shut Kenny's mouth? Throw money at him. In one swoop of a fine ball-point pen, Kenny became the big cheerleading, company man and overall sellout to the new interest. Now it had become clear. All those decisions Kenny was making regarding the crematory, all those mandates Kenny was making where I was concerned, had paid off. *He was now in charge.* Makes sense. Kenny was all about money so he immediately fit in with the corporate model.

The funeral homes and crematory were now corporate-owned. With it came, training classes, OSHA requirements, mandates and guidelines. The public, as always, had no idea that anything had changed. We still had people coming in and regaling us with stories of how they used to go to school with "Donny" and how they knew his old man, yadda, yadda. Appearance stayed the same—mostly. The buildings themselves were put on lockdown. It was common for both funeral homes to have their back doors and garage areas open, convenient for deliveries. Not anymore. Doors were shut and locked. Key codes, cameras and security were put in place. Staff was given marching orders, and new rules and "policing" were becoming commonplace.

Meetings were held. Higher-ups and VPs were greeted, and handshakes given. Pats on the back were administered all for the sole purpose of looking for good places to stick the knives. Like in the case of SCI's "Dignity," we had a new banner. "Share Life." FPG's little corporate tag. To hear the big bosses talk, it was the way we would "service families better." But it soon became clear that the almighty dollar was paramount.

There was this old joke in the funeral industry that SCI, stood for, "Secure Cash Immediately." This was a sort of dig at the money-grubbing corporate feel that the funeral industry was taking on.

We were all told, "Hey, you guys are doing great. We are not out to change anything; we are just partnering with you." In reality, everything was going to change. From increased prices to shifty sales gimmicks, it soon became apparent that if SCI stood for "Secure Cash Immediately" then FPG was an acronym for "Fuck People's Grief."

Our direct disposer business which offered the least expensive cremation in the area and was doing great business, was now under orders to up their price by two-hundred dollars. The funeral homes had undergone the same type of pricing increase, no longer in the interest of staying competitive, simply as a matter of making the most money quickly. I even had to change the way I did business with the outside funeral homes and raise my prices as well. Mandates were given as to whom we bought our urns and caskets from, who was to do the repair work at the crematory and who we would use as vendors and suppliers. I had argued that as long as I was not nitpicked at every turn and told how to run the crematory, I really didn't care. Again, my naivete on the whole matter would bite me in the ass. We had been sold, lock, stock and corpse-filled barrel and the whole atmosphere was becoming a lot worse—everywhere.

CHAPTER 9

Commonly Asked Questions

We now take a little break from my whining about my former career and treat you, the reader, to some of the questions you may have about death, dying and what-ifs. There is a morbid fascination with death. Many times, in my career in the aftercare industry, when people learned what I did for a living, I got one of two reactions. 1) "Ewww, how do you do that? I could never work with dead people…eww!" and 2) "Whoa, that is sooo cool. Wow, that is fascinating, I know this is going to sound weird, but I am fascinated by that…let me ask you some questions if you don't mind." When I told people that I cremated bodies, the look of fascination or disgust was even more pronounced.

I have heard all the dad jokes and comments about my former profession. Things like, "Oh, people are just dying to see you, ha ha" and "Oh wow, do people ever come back to life just for a moment and sit up with their eyes open? What is embalming like? What does burning flesh smell like? Are there ghosts? What is the weirdest thing / grossest thing / craziest thing you have ever witnessed?" This chapter takes a bit of a break from the technical and corporate bullshit of the funeral industry and just really is more for entertainment and to answer some of the questions people have. Even I had some of these questions in my mind before I got into the biz. So here goes.

Before getting into the funeral business, I had seen movies and depictions on television of the funeral industry. Some were purely fiction. No, bodies do not gasp one last breath of air and, with eyelids flailing open, sit upright and scare the bejeezus out of the living. This phenomenon only takes place in movies and is for purely entertainment purposes. I spoke to funeral directors and staff with years of experience behind them when I first ventured into this business, and it remains simply made-up stuff. Do the dead emit sounds or do they move? The short answer is yes. No, they don't sit up but there is air that escapes from a corpse and it can be disconcerting. I have had deceased persons fart upon me, and air has escaped their lungs and it can sound like a bit of a low guttural groan but that is about it.

If you really want to know, I have also had bladders and bowels let loose upon me and have had to shell out a few extra bucks at the dry cleaner, but that is about it. One night, about one in the morning, I was driving about fifty miles back from picking up an elderly woman from a nursing home. She was frail and the removal was an easy one. She weighed, at the time of her death, about ninety pounds. All went well, but it was clear that her final days were difficult ones. So, there I was, with her on the stretcher in the back of the vehicle, driving on a darkened freeway at one in the morning when I changed lanes. She shifted on the stretcher and the sound I heard come from the back of the removal car sounded like this low groan and an exasperated sigh. Now I have had my skill as a driver commented on in the past, but those critiques usually came from passengers who were amongst the living. This experience gave backseat driving an entirely new meaning. Seriously, I had been working in the business all of about a month when this occurred and I almost drove off the road. No one had warned me that this was even a possibility. But there it was. Scared the ever-loving shit out of me. I assure you; she was quite deceased and had been pronounced as such by medical professionals but apparently had some trapped air, and the sound I heard was just that. I got her back to the funeral home and placed her in the embalming room. Again, she was in fact very much dead. She made no further noises.

There are three commonly used methods of disposition: embalming, cremation and direct burial.

In embalming, the blood is drained from the body through the carotid artery and a preservation or embalming fluid is pumped in. The whole process can take forty-five minutes to an hour with no complications, depending on size. Many times, however, there are complications which require further attention. Plastic eye caps are placed in the eyes to give them shape and the mouths are usually wired shut after stuffed with cotton wadding to give shape to the face. The internal organs are drained and a "hardening fluid" is placed in them. Then there is dressing, makeup and placing them into a casket. If you think all of this sounds very invasive, I assure you, it is.

Cremation is disposal by high heat and flame. The deceased is placed in a chamber, one person at a time, and are combusted through means of fire until all that remains are bone and some ash. Those bones are then ground up into a powder with the ash and given back to the families.

Direct burial is just that. There is no embalming. The deceased is dressed, placed into a casket, and buried. There are usually no services and if there are, the deceased is not publicly viewed. It is just a simple burial. Some people choose this method.

Then there are things like organ donation and donating one's body for medical research or other means like forensic study and science. These are things that usually, years earlier, the deceased had made arrangements for, and the family makes sure those wishes are carried out.

Now with the technical stuff out of the way, let me address the dead elephant in the room. The "spooky stuff." There have been those stories floating around the business that there were times when a deceased was brought to the funeral home by mistake. Let me explain. Back in the early days, the sixties and seventies, many funeral homes were contracted to pick up for local medical examiners. They were the ones to go to the car accidents, suicides and homicides. There are some stories that emanate from such pickups. One such story involves a young woman who was in a brutal car accident and was pronounced dead. She was picked up by the local funeral home and taken into their care. Upon placing the woman's naked body upon the cold stainless steel of the embalming table, she gasped and woke up violently. She was in fact still alive, even if just for a brief time. Police and medical pros were called in, and she was in fact still alive but not in great shape. She was taken to a hospital where she did indeed expire. Now, that is one story and I really can't lay claim to the validity of it, but there are stories such as that floating around. Things happen. Mistakes are made, but usually, if there is a whoopsie of that magnitude, it is short-lived and the person in question is in such bad shape that the death is indeed imminent, perhaps just not right then. So, no, people just usually do not spring back to life for one last gasp.

Are there ghosts? Or are funeral homes and crematories haunted? OK, here we go. Now, I preface this one by saying, you believe what you want to believe. Do you believe in life after death? Fine. Do you believe in God, the devil, heaven and hell? Fine. Are you of an atheistic point of view, where there is nothing after we die? That's fine too. I can only approach this question from experiences that I myself have had. I have always believed that there are things that we cannot explain. I have ghost-hunted. I have longed for the sighting of a specter or some proof of an afterworld and perhaps that makes me a bit more "ripe for the picking" a bit more accepting of the unexplained. But here is where I can say that while I have always been open to the notion of ghosts or ghostly happenings, I have also most assuredly experienced them. OK, now you are saying, "I knew it! This guy is a kook and should be locked up!" And perhaps you are ready to close the book and throw it in the corner. But I appeal to you to just hear me out. These are simply unexplained experiences. Read about them and draw your own conclusions.

Again, the short answer is yes. From my point of view, yes, there are ghosts and perhaps there are lingering spirits that are housed at funeral homes. This is my opinion and mine alone. The funeral home at which I was employed had two branches, as I mentioned previously. Branch A is where I worked for several years. Starting with my first night at the funeral home alone with bodies, I really never experienced anything. I could walk up and down the halls and into the various rooms of the establishment and really have no problem. I have napped in the viewing rooms where a body in a casket has been in the corner and I have been in and out of Branch A at all hours, day and night. No issues whatsoever. Branch B, however—I can honestly say that I have always—always—had the feeling that there was someone right behind me or I was being watched whenever I roamed those halls after hours. Sure, perhaps just a feeling. Branch B was actually built and was up and running several years before Branch A but still, there was just something a little off about that place after the lights were out.

At Branch B I heard doors open and shut, I have had that feeling that I was not alone, an overall "creepy" sensation. The crematory was not much better. Now, "experts" will tell you that hauntings happen because the deceased have a fondness for a location or perhaps it is where they expired. That is why hospitals are usually hot spots for such activity. Haunted houses allegedly exist because a former resident had a fondness for the house or it is where they expired. Because of this, it is deemed rare that a funeral home would be haunted. Funeral homes do not bring joy. No one dies at a funeral home. By the time a corpse is wheeled in, they have already died elsewhere and perhaps their "spirit" will live on in those places. But again, I get that hair-on-the-back-of-the-neck creepy feeling at Branch B. I have never been able to pinpoint why.

The crematory—I can tell you most assuredly—yes! I have had things moved on me; I will set something down in a specific spot, only to have it knocked to the floor or moved. There could be explanations for this, but the phone call phenomenon is what really sets the crematory apart. Here is what I mean by that.

In this wonderful technological age, we live in, we all have cell phones and I am no different. I would be on a phone call with my someone and tell them to hold on. I would set the phone down only to return to the phone to the person on the other end asking, "Who are all those people?" When I would inquire as to what they were talking about, the person to whom I was speaking would then tell me, that when I set the phone down, they would hear multiple voices. Voices saying, "Hey!" or "What's this?" or multiple voices talking over one another in an argumentized tone. Creepy, right?

Now, let me take it a bit further. I am a believer in an afterlife. I have a religious faith. But not everyone does. I bring you "Lisa." Lisa was support-staff for the funeral home. A wonderfully kind and free spirit, she danced openly to the beat of her own drum. A hardworking individual with a fascination for the industry. But Lisa is also an atheist. She did not and simply would not adhere to any sort of afterlife hokum. So, again, she is not one to seek out spookies or ghosts.

It is late one summer night, when Lisa arrives at the crematory to drop off a body and place that body in refrigeration. Where the crematory was located was pretty isolated and not well lit. So, for safety's sake, she would have her husband on the phone with her while she took care of what she needed to do. Again, her husband shares her worldview and also is not a believer in the "undead" scenario. She is at the crematory, on the phone with her spouse and needing two hands to perform the next task of placing the deceased int refrigeration, asks her husband to "hold on" and sets the phone down inside the refrigeration unit. She performs her task and comes back to the phone to hear her husband yelling. Her husband is shouting Lisa's name and wanting affirmation that she was ok. Lisa tells him she is fine and asks what his panic is all about.

He asks, "who were those people?"

She asks, "what people?"

"The people all talking over one another, there were several voices!"

Lisa, now a bit freaked, says, "What are you talking about, I am here alone, I assure you, I am by myself."

"That is wild, I heard what sounded like a whole group of people all talking at the same time."

Lisa quickly finished what she was doing and got the hell out of there, keeping her understandably freaked-out husband on the line the entire time. The next day she relayed the story to me. The fact that Lisa is a "nonbeliever" added validity to this story. But that right there shook her and her husband to their core. I remember when she told me the story, I simply grinned and thought, "OK, perhaps I am not losing my mind." I had had similar experiences and now this was, to me, unabashed proof.

It became commonplace for my then-girlfriend to call me at work and tell me, "Oh, there they are again, they are really talkative today." There were times I would be talking to her on the phone in the office and then, still on the phone, walked out to the back where the cooler and the cremator were and she would immediately hear a conversation as if I had just opened the door to a meeting of some sort, only I was alone. She would hear multiple voices and one over the top of them yelling "Hey, hey" or asking, "Who is this?" Is there an explanation? Perhaps, though one has eluded me. There have also been shadows that I cannot explain and things like my shirt being lifted up once—yep, that too has happened—and the occasional sound of the cooler door opening (only for me to investigate and find no one is on the premises except for me). Even the lady who owned the shop next door was not immune to spectral happenings. I found this out when I witnessed her burning sage and waving it about one afternoon. I asked and she explained that apparently, on their security cameras late one night, they caught what appeared to be shadowy translucent figures hanging around the back door of the crematory. She was agitated and was taking her own necessary measures. So, to quote the Cowardly Lion from *The Wizard of Oz*, "I do, I do, I do believe in spooks!"

Now, as far as the most disturbing or grossest thing I have seen goes, I could write a whole other book on this, but let's just say, there is not a lot I haven't seen. I have seen the end result of suicide by shotgun, hanging, and asphyxiation. I have seen the horrors of fire, car accidents and homicides. I have also seen drug overdoses, motorcycle accidents and young lives cut down by their own demons. Here is where I will not go into great detail as to me, these were people. They deserve their privacy and dignity. Period.

Each of these people was someone's husband, wife, daughter, son, someone's loved one and I am not about to go into the horrific details of their demise. Suffice it to say, I have seen the many, many byproducts of death and it is night and day between a 90-year-old Alzheimer sufferer and a hit-and-run victim. It is night and day between an elderly cancer patient and a small child who drowned in a lake. Let me just say that if anyone has ever considered suicide, looking upon the aftereffects of such a death may just put the thought right out of one's head. "Gather ye rosebuds while ye may." No one is promised tomorrow and not one of us gets out of here alive. Those car accident victims, those homicides, even those suicides, were people with hopes, with plans and with dreams. I respect them still and will simply not go into "what is the grossest thing you've seen?"

I took care, great care. From the woman who grabbed my hands and made me promise to put a blanket around her deceased mother in the cooler because "she didn't like the cold" to the family that asked me to "say a prayer" before I cremated their loved one. I took care and I assure you now just as I assured those people then, that I did those things. I was rifling through the linens at 3:00 a.m. at the funeral home just so I could find a blanket, I was reciting the Lord's prayer or the Hail Mary before cremating one of Catholic faith.

These were requests which I took/take seriously. While the funeral directors were concerned about how much money could be made from a contract, I was adhering to seeing that the family took comfort that their loved one was not just another number in my care. I was the last person that this decedent would be with. I was the last one to lay eyes on them. I took everything about this very seriously. To me, it is/was an honor.

I have been asked to include photos with the body or to cremate items that were important to the decedent. Things like teddy bears, cans of beer, cigars or whatever. As I am a sort of cigar aficionado, the most painful thing for me, personally was having to cremate two Cuban cigars with a deceased. Sure, it would have been easy to "procure" these items and simply say that I cremated them with the body, but that was not my bag. I did what was asked of me—*always*. It meant something to these people. It was purely symbolism or a kind gesture, but it meant something to them! In fact, I had one lady bring me flowers because I took care of her young daughter whom had died suddenly. Because I was the last person to lay eyes upon her daughter, I was important to her. We remain friends today. I was important to the family of a young eleven-year-old boy who had passed from a rare form of cancer. They were already friends of mine and because of the service I performed for them, I am now viewed as a part of their family. This is important stuff. Not to be taken lightly or simply as just a job. This means so much to so many people and that is what large corporations are quickly losing sight of.

To those of you whom are looking into the funeral industry as your career, heed my warning. Have compassion. Say something and live up to it. Fuck the bottom line. Show empathy and compassion for those you serve or kindly get the fuck out of the business. I really don't know how much plainer I can make that statement. For there are people, corporations in the funeral industry that are simply a stain on the profession. Those who are not fit to re-pot a plant, let alone lower someone's loved one into a grave. There are those who care only for the money they will make from your sorrow. Be vigilant. Be mindful of this and choose wisely.

CHAPTER 10

Show Me the Money!

This is where I am probably going to piss off a whole lot of people and mind you the people, I will make the angriest are part of the pro capitalist, America-the-land-of-opportunity, what's wrong with-making-a-buck crowd. Let me preface this chapter by simply telling you that I am not antibusiness. I am not anti-money. Nor am I one of those that see money as the root of all evil and that large corporations are the devil. No. But I do believe that the American worker can and should share in a company's success.

There are large corporations that have profit sharing and incentive plans for their workers. Basically, you succeed when the company succeeds. This, I am all for. There are also companies that offer stock options and various benefits to their employees at little or no initial cost. I believe that every successful company out there today owes a large debt of gratitude, first and foremost, to their workers. Those that show up day in and day out, punching in, putting out and punching out to not only put food on their own tables but to ensure the company they work for remains successful and they remain employed.

Too many large corporations today have forgotten what got them to the top of the heap in the first place. We have become a society of gimme, gimme, gimme and when a company is done with you, they are *done*! After World War II, this nation had a way of showing its gratitude toward the men and women who served their country. There are countless stories of corporations and factories helping their employees buy houses, cars and treating their workers with dignity. You see, they knew that if they were going to be successful as a company, they had to treat their workers fairly and as people. Yes, there are also the horror stories as not every large corporation felt this way. Here, I could go into the textile industry, child labor, injured or maimed workers, unfair practices, advantages being taken of workers and the whole reason for the upstart of collective bargaining, worker's rights and labor unions. But there are countless other books on the subject by people far more knowledgeable than I on the subject.

Suffice it to say that when corporations now win, it seems easily forgotten as to why. As I write this, there is a new movement. AI. AI, or artificial intelligence is sweeping corporate America. Robots, machines and computer imaging and programming essentially taking the place of workers. Mixed feelings on this. In one realm, computers and machines are taking jobs from hard working people. On the other hand, the money that companies save on an inflated payroll can be passed along to the consumer and we could very well see a new boom in the United States in the way of manufacturing and the provision of goods and services. But really, where does that leave a skilled labor force? Again, this is not that kind of book. I simply mention this because if you think there are industries and businesses out there that will not be affected, think again.

The funeral home which employed me was sold to a large corporation. This company, from day one seemed bent on one thing and one thing only: acquisition. They seemed to always be boasting about how many more funeral homes they had acquired. They were quick to point out that they were "not trying to be the biggest, simply the best." However, this became difficult to believe when you had several meetings and videos and at the start of the meetings and videos, they would immediately mention how many more funeral homes they had bought. It seemed every week they were purchasing funeral homes, cemeteries and crematories in a variety of new states. Every other month there were new faces, new VPs in charge of this region and that. My attitude going into this new adventure was, "Fine, just leave me the fuck alone." Remember me mentioning earlier as I was increasingly being viewed as "not a team player?" Well, this is where it was becoming more evident. FPG wanted their family conferences to be via zoom or facetime. This, I felt, took the personal touch out of the equation altogether.

Don and Nancy were small business owners. Yes, that business did big business but they were a mom-and-pop shop. You had a beef, go to Don or go to Nancy. Had a purchase that was going to be costly, go to Don or Nancy. Calling in sick, call to your supervisor, Kenny or Carl. It was kind of a big business with a small business vibe and the business was increasingly broken from a worker standpoint.

For instance, we, the employees were required to be on call, as I've discussed. This meant that *our* cell phones that *we* paid for were at *their* disposal. Only the funeral directors got companies cell phones bought and paid for. Also, when we were on call, for the longest time, it was, "be ready to get up, get dressed and get your ass to the funeral home in record time." This expectation was not compensated. If you put your life on hold and stayed home all-night waiting for *your* phone (bought and paid for by you) to ring and you got no call, you made no money. Only in the last year or two that

Don and Nancy owned the company did they relent and see fit to actually pay you to be on call. You got fifty bucks a body when you got a call. If you did not get a call, Don and Nancy saw fit, finally, to give you thirty-five dollars for being on call.

I had fought for years for some type of compensation. I had started working for the funeral home back in the day when cell minutes were part of your cell phone bill. My feeling was, if you were going to expect me to use *my* cell phone, then you should compensate. Too many companies want something for nothing. You see it all the time. And I was not willing to just roll over and take it. Again, not a team player. There were other things, like being asked to work ten, eleven, or twelve hours with no break because some funeral director booked back-to-back services or in the case of running the crematory, being a "one-man-show" and not really being able to take a break and get out for lunch and the like. There is a whole list of things that I really would have pressed compensation on, but again, it seemed a losing battle.

FPG had bought us. As mentioned previously, I was OK with it as long as they left me alone. My attitude was, "if it ain't broke don't fix it." I was encouraged, however, as it now a corporate shop, we would have an HR department. The workplace bullshit and bullying that had gone on for years would now come to an end. We would have structure. We would have a tighter-run-ship so to speak. Something that this organization needed. I was not that concerned. I did my job and did it well. For the most part we had some good employees but also some, well, not so good. I was really hoping the miscommunication that Kenny was so adept at would come to an end. With FPG making him a "lead" I am sure things would be better as far as Kenny and all of his ineptness was concerned. Perhaps ole Kenny would step up his game. Actually, Kenny did adapt to the new environment and even would reach out to everyone and see how things were going and offer help when he could. But there is an old saying. If you sober up a horse thief, all you have at the end of a day is a sober horse thief. This applied to Kenny.

Kenny was still a communication nightmare. He had dropped the ball so many times, and he and his minions had gotten our organization damn near sued so many times it isn't funny. His laissez-faire approach to managing was abysmal as an FDIC, so his being knighted and made a lead only meant that the fuck ups would happen at a higher level and blame was easier to place.

Again, as long as they left me alone, I really didn't care. But, come on, who was I kidding? They were not about to do that. I was their property. Just like the equipment, the files, right down to the stapler on my desk. I was another acquisition. They started with my vendors. They started to dictate who was going to handle our recycling and who was going to be doing repairs. From there it moved on to who was going to do the refractory work, who was going to handle my office supplies, how payments would be taken. That of course resulted in an increase in prices for outside funeral homes and new cremation authorization forms that *their* families had to sign. Eventually they got around to me and how I was going to do my job, A job I had been doing excellently for eight years.

Prior to purchasing us, FPG had bought another funeral home and crematory in the area and now they were going to shutter that crematory and move their cases and their trade funeral homes to me. Further, though this crematory was also part of FPG, they had not been playing by the rules. They were not charging what I had been told to charge, nor had they been doing business the same way. So here came all of their outside funeral homes, some of which had left me when we had the price increase. Here they were, coming back to me—the asshole—the guy who charged too much and had rules. What these funeral homes did not know was, I fought the price increase and the added paperwork, I fought for them, but was told, "Do it or else." Meanwhile, there were other firms owned by FPG doing their own thing and getting by with it.

Now, the twelve outside funeral homes I was cremating for was turning to sixteen. I was then told that it would be expected of me to do no less than ten bodies per day and to do all of "our" cases first. In other words, I was to cremate all of our funeral home's cases and our direct disposer cases and leave the trade cases for last. The problem with FPG soon became apparent. FPG hired men and women whom had never been in the industry before. They had no clue about the funeral industry and if I tried to explain something it was like trying to read Shakespeare to a dog. A lot of blank looks and head tilting.

I was already working eight to eleven hours a day cremating for our funeral homes and the outside funeral homes. I was beyond busy. I would come in at seven and leave at five or six. Now, they were going to pile on more work and higher expectations and I was to keep it all under forty hours a week. Again, I was a one-man-show. They were stacking on four more funeral homes on top of me and now I had "higher-ups" telling me *how* to do my job. They had cut me down to a four-day work week (four ten-hour days), and if I didn't take a lunch, I had better have a damned good explanation as to why. At the end of a year under the FPG banner we saw major changes. Everyone's workload had increased, *all* of our prices had increased, our direct disposer could no longer boast that it offered the least-expensive cremation, everything from where we bought our caskets to our security company had changed. Everyday brought with it new and bizarre challenges.

Their goal was to make my crematory the "central crematory" for the company. So, when they shuttered the crematory over in the next town and my workload increased, they did so as a "cost-saving measure." Only, this made no sense. They now had to hire people to transport bodies from that location over to me. They were always in desperate need for support staff, or "funeral attendants" as they were now called. The train was starting to come off the rails and it became very apparent that FPG really cared nothing about their employees but more about the almighty dollar.

During this time, I had started to face more backlash. The funeral homes had stopped talking to me altogether. I was simply a fixture, someone they *had* to deal with from time to time. One of the funeral directors and I had had some words when she attempted to order me around like some lacky. I contacted HR. They did nothing. So much for my "tighter ship" theory. They simply responded with an automated email and an automated phone call. It was laughable.

After a year being owned by FPG, we all were asking the same question: What about raises? Under private ownership, we were given, at very least, a cost-of-living increase. Sometimes it would be more; sometimes it would be less. Then there were things like Christmas bonuses and various other incentives. But not under this regime! As I write this, it has now been two years under corporate ownership and I am told by some employees there that raises are nowhere in sight.

With the nitpicking, vendor changes, and now a ridiculously increased workload, I was starting to ask on a weekly basis about an increase in pay. They expected a whole hell of a lot more out of me, but every time I asked for more it was met with stuttering, and a lot of ums and uhs and "We are looking into it…soon…I promise." The fact was, there were not going to be any raises. Not for me or anyone else. Well, almost. You remember Dara? The one whom Kenny thought that the Sun rose and set by? Yep, she got a raise. Meanwhile, everyone else could go fuck themselves. Not one other person saw an increase in pay. Everyone saw a lot more work, however.

We all were busting ass. As for me, I was up to my eyeballs in outside funeral homes and it was getting to me. I was also still unable to take any sort of vacation. I needed backup. I needed help. But I saw how understaffed the funeral homes were and how their pleas for more help were falling on deaf ears, so I knew I was screwed. FPG had started to make big plans for the crematory. They wanted me to "be involved." Again, I was drowning in the job. I was working my four ten-hour days and it was all I could do to cremate for the funeral homes, the outside funeral homes and the direct disposer business. I was cremating ten bodies a day and being questioned and given the third degree when I didn't. From day one, I said, you want to be a corporate shop? Fine, just leave me to do my job. Pay me fairly and leave me alone. Who was I to expect or even think that this would be the case? The more I pulled the more they pushed. Then, I became one of their customers.

CHAPTER 11

What about When I Needed You?

My stepfather was a great guy. I had lost my biological father when I was five, the man whom I would come to consider my stepfather was a hard-working, self-made man who had made some wise investments and business ventures. Into his late seventies he had started to develop some serious health issues. He was falling more and was becoming more feeble and more dependent on a cane or walker. Since I was his only family in the area, he relied upon me for a variety of things. Everything from changing a light bulb to helping with doctor's visits, he relied upon me. He would soon take a fall in 2021 and sustain an injury that would become terribly infected. He then developed pneumonia and would be on and off of a ventilator. It was during this time that I would learn I was his power of attorney and would be executor of his estate. This came as a surprise to me as he had other family, albeit in other parts of the country. Nonetheless, it would be a task that I would undertake as best I could—for him.

Three times he went on a ventilator and three times the doctors pushed palliative care on me. That would mean he would have to be transported to a facility fifty miles away and placed on a feeding tube and breathing machine as his lungs were too weak. I knew my stepfather. I knew what he wanted, and if there was any doubt, there was a twenty-page document provided by his attorney that outlined what he wanted. I read every line. Then I read it again and again and again. I consulted with doctors and his sister and brother-in-law. An ultimate decision was mine and I didn't want it to be, but there came a time when I had to make it. He was not getting better and would not get better unless on machines. He didn't want that. I knew he didn't and it was stated in the living will that he did not want that. I already had him placed on ventilation more times than he would have wanted. I had to let him go.

I made the decision on March 10 to have him taken off the support. On March 12, at noon, he passed peacefully. I was devastated. Having lost my mother ten years earlier, this was equally as difficult. Moreso because I had to make the call. Just like ten years prior, consulting with doctors and hospice about my mother. This kind of thing never get easier. Those of you whom have lost a parent know how difficult it is. But now, he was gone and I had to rely upon my business to take care of him.

Several months prior I had talked him into prearranging his funeral arrangements. That way, there would be no questions when the time came as to what he wanted. He sat down with one of our prearrangement counselors and got everything bought and paid for. He was a veteran, so he could be interred at a national cemetery. He wanted no fuss, no embalming, simply a direct burial at a national cemetery. Cut-and-dried. No services, no honors no nothing. Just direct burial at a National Cemetery. I was familiar with this type of request, so I was going to make sure his wishes were honored.

My stepfather had passed and I was called by the hospital; they asked if I had selected a funeral home. The answer was a resounding yes. Thankfully, my stepfather had his preneed in order and I told them of the funeral home handling things. The next phone call I received was from my oh-so-favorite staff member, Dara. I told Dara that he was my stepfather; she was kind and offered her condolences. I relayed to her that he would in fact be a direct burial at a well-known national cemetery. Again, Dara understood and said she would have him picked up and brought to the funeral home. Now, this is one area of the job I could never perform. I had cremated family and friends in the past. I had known many people whom I would later cremate and to me, it was always an honor. But the one thing I myself could never do was to go and pick up my deceased family member myself. I wanted to remember them as they were. I wanted to have my final memory of them not be me sliding them onto a stretcher and wheeling them down a hallway and into the back of a waiting vehicle. I always left that particular task to those we paid to do just that. He was picked up on that Saturday on which he passed and placed in refrigeration. This man, who took me to my first ball game, this man whom I went fishing with, whom had brought my mother so much joy was now gone. He served his country and he was a good and decent, honorable individual and now I was entrusted with carrying out his wishes.

My son, had taken a job with the funeral home several years prior. He had become the licensed direct disposer for the direct disposer company that Don and Nancy had started. So, yes, I worked with my son and he was going a lot further than his old man ever went in the business and now my stepfather, his grandfather, was in the care of the funeral home that employed us. As mentioned, my stepfather wanted no fuss. Simply a direct burial. Again, Kenny and Dara were involved and what happened next is one more reason I chose to write this book as a warning to others.

My son and I had made up our minds that *we* would be the ones to take my stepfather to his final resting place. A "drop-in" as it is called, is when there is no service or procession. You show up at the cemetery with a permit and the deceased and you take him to the gravesite. You are then met by the cemetery staff and you hand over the casket. They do the rest. Then you leave. We were going to hang around and watch him lowered into the ground. It was the least that we could do for a man whom was so good to both my son and I. But the days leading up to this were days filled with, again, miscommunication and I was treated as little more than a bother.

First, Kenny had failed to contact me about any of the process. One of our phone conversations he had flippantly stated that my stepfather needed clothes and I should bring those to the funeral home. But Kenny was very clear on the charges for things like the obituary and the costs of death certificates, things that were not pre-paid. I made sure the clothing got over to the funeral home and we discussed what day the drop-in would occur. It was set for a Monday morning. My son and I got to the funeral home to find that my stepfather had not yet been placed in his casket. He was not ready to go in other words. When we arrived at the funeral home, first thing that Monday morning, I asked where my stepfather was. Dara snapped at me.

"He is still in the cooler. He's not embalmed you know; he is a direct burial!"

I responded, "Oh, well, I thought he would have been in the casket at least so I could see him. I have some items to go in with him."

"No, he isn't! He is a direct burial. We don't have him in the casket yet!"

I thought, "Wow, I hope she doesn't treat all grieving families like the way she is treating me right now."

My son, showed up at that point, and one of the administrators had come up to me and commented on how "bad" my stepfather looked. "He looks really bad" was how it was put to me.

"Yes," I responded, "he has been on a ventilator for about three weeks; he is not going to look that great. I know."

Again, I was amazed at just how I was being spoken to. I had worked with these people for years and they were making these comments and quite frankly being quite rude about it instead of thinking for a moment and realizing that *I was a fucking customer.* I was a bereaved client. I deserved whatever respect they could possibly muster at that point.

I turned to my son and informed him that he was not ready yet. My son got this look on his face as if to say, "Would it have killed them to come in a bit early and have him ready? You know…for us?"

Nope, instead, they went to the cooler, wheeled him out and headed to the prep room with him to get him into the casket. My son, the class act that he is, went in to help. My son helped place his grandfather into a casket, all while listening to Kenny and anyone else in the prep room comment on how bad his grandfather looked.

"Oh, he looks really bad. Wow, he has to be one hundred pounds. Oh man he looks bad" and other comments were made in the presence of my son who was simply there to make sure he got placed in the casket with the dignity he deserved.

My son came out of the prep room, helping wheel the casket into the garage area. He was visibly shaken and a bit upset. I had brought some photos and some oranges from my stepfather's orange trees that he took so much pride in. I went over to open the lid of the casket only to find it had been locked down already. Fuck! The whole reason I showed up as early as I did was to view my stepfather one last time, in his casket and place these items in with him. All *they* were worried about was getting him out of there. I turned to Kenny and said, "The casket is already locked down? I did want to see him and place these items in with him...hello?"

Kenny retorted, "Oh." He laughed. "We thought you were ready to go, we locked it down." Exasperated, he added, "We will open it back up for ya."

Again, my head was spinning, it seemed that for the simple act of looking upon the face of the man who helped raise me, I was a bother. I was growing angrier by the minute.

They opened the casket; indeed, my stepfather had looked better. But that was for *me* to judge and *me* alone. I carefully placed the items in the casket as they all stood around seemingly waiting for me to finish. I simply wanted a moment alone with this man. My son wanted that too. But it seemed to simply be an afterthought with my esteemed coworkers. They just wanted him gone, wanted us gone. I felt pangs of sadness hit me and tears come to my eyes. At that point, I would *not* let those bastards see me cry. We closed the casket and finished loading him into the back of the GMC Yukon to take to the cemetery.

In the weeks and months that followed, I would read reviews sent out by FPG and their marketing division on how Dara was so kind, how she was wonderful and so easy to talk to. My thought was, "Dara who?" She sure as fuck wasn't so kind with me. That whole debacle with my stepfather was proof positive that Dara, and Kenny for that matter, should stay clear of grieving families forever.

He deserved a flag and was entitled to one. It would be seven months before I ever got that. When I brought it to Kenny's attention his response was, "Come get it if you want it." I refused.

My thought was, "No, you ass-bag, you *bring* it to me!" I would get one brought to me by Mary from Branch B. It went like this. Kenny didn't want to make sure all the t's were crossed and i's were dotted on my stepfather's services, so he just picked up the phone, called branch B, which was closer in proximity to the crematory and told them to "give me a flag." He clearly could not be bothered.

Funerals are big business and the dollars and cents add up. The funeral homes were making a lot of money. Every time someone dies, Kenny gets to go on a cruise. The caring part of the funeral industry, the reason I got into this business in the first place, no longer existed. When I needed compassion, I was a bother. When I expected respect, there was none to be had. My stepfather is resting comfortably at a national cemetery. I honored his wishes and I made sure they were carried out. My son, helped his grandfather to procure that dignified burial as well.

My stepfather never cared for cremation and had commented that he didn't know how I could do that job. He wanted to be interred at a national cemetery. I made sure that that took place. But if his wishes *had* been to be cremated, I tell you this: I would have made damn sure he was treated with a hell of a lot more honor and respect than he received at the funeral home.

This brought to mind the fact that years earlier, when my mother was dying, I was given a hard time for taking "an extended lunch" because the nursing home she was in was ten miles away and I would visit her daily. Then when she passed, I had to beg on bended knee for the time off to inter her ashes in another state. It wasn't just me either. There was another support staff gentleman with whom I worked. His mother passed. He was absolutely inconsolable. He needed some time off. The attitude at the funeral home? "Can't he just get over it?" It seemed, as employees of this industry, we were expected to just shake off our grief when death visits us.

It boggles my mind. Kenny is a former marine. Don is too. They have shown immense respect for veterans in their care. They arranged many times for the honor guard and the playing of taps. They saluted flag-draped caskets and made sure that those who served their country were honored in their funeral. My stepfather was a Vietnam veteran. But he simply chose a quiet private burial instead of all the pomp and circumstance. I was proud to make sure his wishes were carried out. Meanwhile, my coworkers were just moving him about and so damned in a hurry they couldn't even give me a moment or two with him. My son and I carried out his wishes but we were rushed out the door in doing so. I was growing weary of the whole business end of the business and growing increasingly tired of those self-proclaimed professionals I worked for and with. I was on the way toward the door for the last time.

CHAPTER 12

You Might Want to Know Your Business

have some advice. There is an old saying, "Those who cannot do, teach." So let me preface this by saying that I am not a businessman. I do not own, nor have I ever owned, a business. I have not been a CEO, CFO, VP or anything of this nature. I have been in management, and I have had to "calm the waters of discontent" from time to time. I would not classify myself as a people person and can be, at times, the worst nightmare for human resource departments, as I am apt, as evidenced in this book, to speak my mind. With that said, I do have some advice for those about to acquire funeral homes in a mad cash grab. Know the business you are about to become a part of.

My whole problem with large corporations is that they tend to put people in charge who have never been in the relevant type of business before. For instance, I worked years ago for a safety supply company whose CEO was very concerned about the bottom line. Money, money, money! This particular CEO came from the restaurant industry having headed up a major chain of nationally renowned restaurants, and now here he was, a major player in the workplace safety game. Look, I get it, business is business. You want your company to make the most money at the end of the day and the overall formula for doing so may be basically the same across industries. However, when you are dealing with people—I mean real goddamned *people*—you need to slow your roll. Let us address the elephant in the room. How does the funeral industry make its money? From *your* grief. Period!

Your mother has passed away at eighty-eight. You are grieving the loss of such a powerful force in your life and the life of your family. You never wanted to think about this day. You never wanted to talk about it. Nobody really does. But now the day has arrived and you must carry out her funeral in a dignified and caring way. "Who will take care of them?" is the first question that comes to mind and it is usually answered haphazardly. You choose the big funeral home with the big parking lot and the professional-looking staff. Maybe you have heard good things, maybe you attended a funeral or two there, or maybe, just maybe you are so lost and so grief-stricken that you are making the decision on the fly. No research, no pre-arrangement—you are making a spur-of-the-moment decision on what will likely cost you thousands if there was no sort of insurance. *That* is what these big funeral homes are counting on. Get 'em in. Get the money. Get 'em out. "Next!"

The big corporations are banking on your grief. Remember that earlier I pointed to the fact that the old-fashioned mom-and-pop funeral home no longer exist in many cities across this country? How these "caring funeral establishments" are now just a part of the corporate machine? Well, it is true. Once or twice a week, that funeral home where your dear mother is laying, has to report the P&L for the week or month. They answer to a higher calling. Some number-crunching controller or CEO wanting to know why you had a contract for $8,000 when you could have easily bilked that family for $10,000.

If your mom is to be buried, they will show you the stainless steel or bronze caskets. Don't get me started on the mark ups on those things. Suffice to say, it is substantial. Also, that friendly, soft-spoken funeral director is really nothing more than a glorified salesperson, employed by you to take care of what needs to be taken care of. You are essentially at their mercy. It's like driving onto a car lot in your car that is clearly on its last leg. Smoke is pouring out the back; it is backfiring and almost stalling. You almost have to push the damned thing into the lot. It is very clear you *need* a car, right now. Well, in the funeral game, you are trapped kind of in the same way.

Sure, there are other funeral homes, but the one you are at now is where your mother is already housed. She was picked up last night and brought to *this* funeral home. Sure, you could go elsewhere, but number 1) you would probably wind up taking her to another soul-sucking corporate funeral home or 2) you would have to pay two or three hundred for the pickup and transport of her earthly remains in order to have her released to another funeral home. Then there is the possibility that you may not want to do business with this establishment and choose another funeral home only to find out they are part of the same company. Yep, it happens. So, you are trapped, and that is exactly how these big corporations want it. You are trapped, you *need* their services and they are going to see that you do not exit their location until you have signed a contract for the big fat costly service. They will even remind you they take all credit cards.

The CEOs and VPs all want that money. They want the fat contracts and they really couldn't care less about you or your mother. It becomes a big money grab. That is why so many of these executives come from other industries. In their former companies, it was about sales, money, bottom line. In the funeral industry, the big multibillion-dollar death care industry, it is the same way. But wait. What about that grieving family? What about that young mother whose son has just died in a horrific car accident? What about the sympathy, the empathy? Oh, they will show it as long as you sign on the dotted line. The funeral industry in this country has become the same old numbers game like every other business and there are those in the industry who are out for the big payday and that is it.

The morning that I went to pick up my stepfather, I saw it. He had prearranged. He had paid for his services in full. They already had their money so when it came to showing me some kindness and compassion, they felt they didn't need to. After all, who was I? I was their coworker; I was this guy whom they had worked with for years. Kenny even pointed out that he "made sure to get him a better casket than the one he paid for." At that point, I didn't give two shits about that. I wanted to be shown some compassion. I wanted my grief to be recognized. I realize I am droning on about this, but there is really nothing that could have prepared me for how I was treated by my coworkers that morning.

When we think of big business in this country or around the world for that matter, we think of the major players, Ford, GM, Amazon, Walmart, the major corporations we see on the news day in and day out. But the Death Care industry is every bit as big and getting bigger by the minute. It just isn't talked about as much. Yet they continue to employ bean-counting imbeciles and placing them at the top of the food chain in these companies.

At the crematory, I had my fair share of these "execs" come in and start telling me how to do the job. They would tell me what was expected. They would instruct me on who I should cremate first.

We butted heads. I was getting the job done and here they were telling me on how many I needed to do, how they could make the most money and save them the most at the same time. It was becoming clear to me that when I would try to explain how the whole thing worked and how there were state guidelines we had to adhere to, it was lost on them. Numbers, numbers, numbers. That is what it came down to.

I had told myself a long time ago that when the people I was cremating became nameless, faceless numbers to me, when my own empathy betrayed me, when all I cared about was how much I could do, how many people I could cremate, when it became about numbers to me, then it was time to go. It was becoming just that. Numbers.

People were no longer people to me. They had become nameless, faceless numbers. There was this need, this requirement, to cremate, cremate, cremate. Get 'em in, get 'em out. I was becoming exactly what the corporation wanted me to be. I was doing exactly what was required and started to view things like "special requests" as pains in the ass. What? You want a fingerprint? you want a picture or some memento cremated with them? You want a lock of hair? You want me to say a prayer? Well, ok, so long as it doesn't take up a lot of time. I have a schedule to keep! Your granny, your husband, your child is just one of ten I have to get done for the day. Don't harsh my flow. Don't bug me with your wants and wishes.

What the hell happened? I was the caring one. I was the one who was going to be the last person this decedent would be with. That which I viewed as an honor was now becoming a bother or a nuisance. I was becoming this—thing— this unfeeling corpse pyromaniac. I was becoming all that I despised. To the company, I was an asset. I was a backbreaking, hardworking cog in the machine, as long as I was a good boy and took my lunch and didn't go over forty hours. I was to obey, not ask questions and just burn these people. It had become time to honor the promise I had made to myself. It was time to say enough and leave the business I thought I knew.

CHAPTER 13

Death and Social Media (And Knowing When to Leave)

There was a show on the Discovery Channel a while back. *Dr. G: Medical Examiner.* This show depicted the behind-the-scenes of an Orange County, Florida, medical examiner. Dr. Garavaglia or Dr. G, a forensic expert in her field. She had more than once graced the witness stand of some very high-profile cases and her word as a top medical scientist was untarnished. She had been working in Central Florida for many years when a television producer began to think it would be an educational, sensational idea to put her front and center with a television show that showed the other aspect of what happens when you die. I jokingly called it ATV, Autopsy Television. I watched it quite a few times and found it extremely informative. Dr. G was a class act and never once let the presence of a camera sensationalize or overdramatize what she did for a living. Something interesting happened through the broadcast of this show. It fostered a renewed interest in forensics and attracted a great many people, young women especially, into the field.

Meanwhile, *Law and Order, CSI* and other fictional crime shows tend to insist that when a person is murdered, within a few days, there is a mountain of forensic evidence, complete with a full toxicology report, and an arrest is made. Case closed! In reality, it is a bit more complex than that. A typical toxicology screen done by the medical examiner can take weeks or months to conclude. There is also tissue analysis and microscopic examination, which all take a lot of time, to help determine just what the hell happened to cause this person's demise. It is science. People like Dr. Garavaglia are highly trained, highly skilled professionals whose education is vast and ongoing. They are the *real* people in the morgues and up to their elbows in organs and chest cavities in order to determine outcomes and causes.

CSI, Law & Order and shows like them only have an hour or two to tell their stories and wrap up any loose ends. It is important to discern between fiction and reality. *CSI* is fiction and the only thing shows like it accomplishes is causing real-life families to wonder why it is taking so long to get a cause of death from a medical examiner. Forensics are science. I have seen medical examiners send police officers to impound lots or junk yards to scour the back seat of a wrecked car for a piece of skull or fragment of brain. I have viewed autopsies. I have viewed forensic photos, witnessed fingernail scrapings and hair follicle analysis. It is science. It takes time. But all this to say that TV is for entertainment and it seems that death is playing a large part in that realm.

Between true crime podcasts, murder shows and serial killer biopics, the fascination with people like John Wayne Gacy, Charles Manson, Ted Bundy and their victims keep people glued to their electronic devices. Why is that? Perhaps unlike those on *CSI* and *Law & Order*, these are real cases, grabbed from history and headlines. Bundy, Dahmer, H.H. Holmes (Google him) draw people in. Crime, particularly crimes involving multiple homicides, capture the imagination. People seem to enjoy death and the stories behind them. The "what went wrong" of it all.

As for the ever-growing field of social media, there is certainly no shortage of death talk there either. There are a number of Tik Tokers and YouTubers out there right now who are making a name for themselves by talking death. There is the hospice nurse who talks candidly about the final moments of a person's life and the act of dying. Then there is the smartly dressed young female funeral director who tells witty little anecdotes about the behind-the-scenes stuff at funeral homes and crematories. There are the "vault guys" who show step-by-step what goes into installing a cemetery vault for burial, the medical examiner who performs autopsies and so on. These are just a few examples of people who are answering questions and educating in a well-meaning manner. I believe these people are well-intentioned but I also believe there are those out there who make it all about themselves.

In essence, they are saying "Hey, look at me, I deal in death. Ain't that cool?" more than simply doing it for educational purposes. They are searching the spotlight by talking about their craft. Can't blame them—people are fascinated by death, and they have found a niche. Hey, I guess I am guilty of that too. I am, after all, writing this book. But when you watch these "professionals" there is something you need to keep in mind. You need to ask yourself, why? What is this fascination with death? The smartly dressed funeral director talking about embalming or cremation is entertaining to you. Why? Because we are intrigued by that which we fear, that which we know nothing about and hell, it makes for some interesting stories.

We watch Mike Rowe and the show *Dirty Jobs* for somewhat the same reason. We find it interesting to learn about jobs we never really thought about before. The funeral industry—oooh, now that is cool because it has that oogy, icky, spooky factor. But it is important to realize and always remember that when that Tik Tok funeral director is talking about embalming or cremation, they are talking about a service they perform for *people* on *people*. The job must be more than a "job." Why do you find it entertaining? It all, after a while, becomes entertainment and if you are watching these videos and Tik Toks, you have to ask yourself why, and from that why, perhaps you too may consider a career in the field, as did I.

I admit, I always had a fascination with death and it was brought to the surface when A&E network had a show called *Family Plots*. This show followed a family in the funeral business; they owned the Poway Bernardo Mortuary in California. The show concentrated on the behind-the-scenes drama and personalities of the staff at the establishment and gave a view into people simply doing their jobs. An unusual job, granted, but one that must be done. It showed that even funeral professionals are not immune to interoffice squabbling and arguments and drama, like every other workplace. It humanized the industry for me and piqued my interest.

Still today there are several shows and series depicting the "real-life death industry." There is *Buried by the Bernards*, on Netflix, which depicts the behind the scenes of a well-known family-owned firm in Memphis, Tennessee. *The Casketeers*, is a really cool show all about funeral professionals in New Zealand and the various customs and traditions that they must contend with. There is also a three-part series about different UK traditions, customs and funeral professionals. Lastly, there are shows that will simply touch on the subject. For example, Adam Conover's show, *Adam Ruins Everything* got into the act with an episode that spoke very candidly about the industry. This episode is a personal favorite because in it, Adam calls out big corporate like SCI and talks about some interesting practices. All of these shows are interesting and informative and I believe it is always a good thing to learn about various customs, traditions, and behind-the-scenes material as much as possible. Especially if you are looking into a career in mortuary.

Fictional shows about the deathcare industry are very popular as well. Remember the hit HBO series, *Six Feet Under*, which started every episode with a horrific death or freak accident? Even light-hearted comedies like *The Munsters* were not above getting in on the act with Herman being employed by the Goodbury and Graves Funeral Parlor. Death has always had a bit of entertainment factor to it.

Then there are true stories made into movies. As I write this, a new movie has hit Amazon Prime. *The Burial*. It tells the story of a small-town Mississippi funeral director who goes head-to-head with a corporate conglomerate in court after being swindled. A sort of unflattering depiction of the large corporate mindset. Here, we come full circle and back into the catalyst for this book.

Death is a fact of life. We will all face it and we have already faced it with the loss of loved ones and friends. I believe it is that common thread that really sparks the fascination. It is something we *all* will go through and there is a multibillion industry in this country that is banking on that. Your death will benefit some fat-cat corporation and their shareholders. Some funeral "professional" is going to make bank off your flesh. It is a fact and I truly believe that if there is one facet of life that large corporations are cheapening and muddying, it is death. A business that has been built on compassion, empathy and service has become anything but.

Corporations have systematically reached in and yanked out empathy and compassion and replaced it with a healthy bottom-line.

That is the real reason I got out. Every week, I had started to scope out *how many, how much* I could get done. I had become the drone that FPG wanted me to become. Dan and Nancy got out; they sold to the highest bidder, rode off into the sunset with a big fat check and assured us all that FPG was a different kind of company, that they cared and there was nothing to worry about— they lied.

As we have seen, FPG immediately started raising prices, shifting people, changing the product, and essentially forgetting that the product of the funeral industry should be compassion. But then again, you really can't make money off of caring, can you? Hey, business is business. When it was independently owned, Don wanted "meat on the table." Meaning, he wanted the bodies on the prep room table to be embalmed because that meant the casket, the service, the grave, the big money funeral. FPG, wants that too, but it is so much easier to just raise prices across the board. Burials, caskets, even cremation all go up and the employees still are not being compensated. They want the work and the profits.

Here is where I become really unpopular. I truly do believe that the funeral industry needs to unionize. As more big corporations gobble up funeral homes and wait for those baby boomers to kick off, they are working their staff to the bone (again, pun). As the funeral professionals work harder, on call, overtime (when permitted of course) spending six or seven days working, working, working with little or no compensation, the funeral pro is becoming fatigued. They are caring less, they are unhappy in their chosen profession and when it comes time to care—they are tapped out. It was happening to me.

I was a one man show at the crematory. I couldn't take a break; I couldn't take a vacation. Near the end, I even told my "superiors" that I was one injury or serious illness from them being totally screwed! If I was off for anytime, I had to work twice as hard to get caught up. Caring? Who had time for that? I had a certain number to cremate. Burnout was becoming very real.

Let's talk about that. The funeral director who has been meeting with families, performing services, sometimes back-to-back and now is on his sixth day in row working, has got to embalm Mr. Jones. But he is so exhausted that one slip of the scalpel could mean the end of his career. There are health risks and dangers in the industry. Funeral directors—support staff—crematory ops—everyone—needs to be protected, compensated and not just treated like a worker drone.

I knew I was spent. I was suffering from partial hearing loss, shoulder, back problems and exhaustion. I either had to make a change or be found face down at the crematory. The people still working at the funeral home are working their asses off and for what? Really, for what? Meanwhile people like Kenny and the brain-dead executives go about their *business* doing *business* and comparing their numbers and contract amounts to other funeral homes and when that dear little old lady walks in the front door after having lost her husband of sixty years, all they see is a big fat dollar sign. That is what the business has become. Again, grief equals a big payday for these large corporate funeral homes.

I realize that it is somewhat two-faced for me to complain that all these big corporations cared about was money and then in the same breath, complain that I and my colleagues had not seen a raise since being bought out. But it was becoming evident that the money that FPG cared most about was the money they had coming in (contracts/deaths), *not* the money they had going out (payroll). Oh, don't get me wrong, it's not just big scary corporations that are guilty of this. I see it in small business as well. You work your staff to death and expect top service from them but you don't want to take care of them financially, so you have this big group of very unhappy employees wishing for *your* death.

I am simply saying that large corporations are most guilty of this because, let's face it, they *have* the money. I am more apt to forgive the small businessman of this behavior as he is just that, a small business. But the Amazons, Walmart's, and Apples of the world—and for that matter, the funeral corporations—could loosen the purse strings a little when it comes to staff. Here is a news flash for ya. Compensation equals happy employees. Protected workers, at the very least, employees who feel respected. Shocker, I know, right? Maybe, that funeral director or hospice nurse on Tik Tok ought to cover that as a topic.

It was becoming quite clear that this large corporation that owned us wanted what all large corporations want: double or triple the work at the same rate of pay. That is what it finally came down to. I was expected to take on more work (six more funeral homes to cremate for) more responsibility, have virtually no say in how the crematory was run, and then I was not be compensated for that extra work and effort. Also, they expected this extra workload to all fit within that forty-hour workweek. It was time to go, and fortunately I was in a position where I could leave. I spoke with my boss at FPG and we discussed money and what it would take to make me stay. No agreement was made, so we parted ways. I gave my two weeks' notice and finished out those two weeks.

Fortunately, through my recommendation, they had found someone to take the helm. I had spent the last few weeks training this person and felt confident that the crematory I had worked so hard to make the very best would be left in capable hands. My last day came and by the end of that day, I had an epiphany. After fifteen years of hard work and dedication, after all that I had done, how hard I had worked, not one single person wished me well or told me goodbye. See how popular I had become? Not one. No one wished me luck, told me they would miss me, said a fond farewell, goodbye, fuck you, *nothing*. By 4:00 p.m. that day, If I was ever in doubt whether it was the right time to leave, it was most assuredly confirmed that it was.

In the following days, FPG would wipe out the computer system that held key information and essential paperwork that my successor needed. In other words, they took a baton and kneecapped the person following me. When this person tried to explain the situation, they told her to "shut up and stop whining." Wow, professional! Words were exchanged and that person left, then there was another person and then another. Again, those in charge had never worked in the funeral industry, so they started putting Band-Aids and duct tape on procedure and started doing some shady stuff all in the name of "getting by."

Certificates were being made and signed by people *not* actually performing the cremation, cremations were taking place without the necessary documents in hand, larger cases were being loaded in and cremated at a variety of different times throughout the day, putting safety at risk, and other things. At this writing, it has been six months since I left and I have it on authority that the crematory is back to being an unorganized, lost entity, run by someone whom means well, but is inadequately trained. I can only guess, when a state inspection rolls around, they may be in some trouble. Perhaps Kenny should call the state and report *his own company*.

CHAPTER 14

So, Now What?

In these pages I have illustrated the good, the bad and the ugly of what was once, a very time-honored and noble profession. I have regaled you with anecdotes and stories of some people who are working in this industry. While a bit hypercritical at times, I admit that while I am not a funeral director, those things which I have witnessed in this field should be viewed as a warning to not only the customer but to those who still ply this trade. There is a very large lucrative business out there that is getting larger and more lucrative by the number of tears you shed. Maybe they come to you in a suit and tie or maybe a pair of khakis and a smart polo shirt, but the patter is always the same. "They care." They care about you, and they care about your loved one. In reality, this is true—partly. They do care. They care about how much you are going to spend. The old-timey-family-run funeral home is quickly becoming a thing of the past and little more than a cover-up for a big corporation.

What do you do when your loved one dies and you are face to face with that funeral director? Here are some questions you need to ask:

- Are you a corporate run funeral home?
- May I tour your facility and meet your staff?
- Do you own your own crematory?
- Seriously, what can I expect to pay? Ballpark is fine.

- How long have you been in business. (if corporate, how long has this corporation owned this facility?)
- Do you offer grief counseling?
- If I choose not to do business with you, may I have my loved one transported elsewhere and how much is it to do that?

Now, that last question is one that frightens funeral homes. They want your business; they want your money. If they went out to pick your loved one up it is because of a few reasons. Your loved one made prearrangements for this facility to do the service. The hospital or nursing home called "a funeral home, any funeral home" because one was not clearly stated on paperwork. Or in the case of someone dying at home, the next funeral home on the rotation list was called.

So, you sit down with the funeral professional. Maybe you don't like him or her. Maybe you are unimpressed with the facility. Maybe, just maybe, you get that used car dealership vibe. This is where you can most certainly go elsewhere. You can call another funeral home and have your loved one transported there. It is perfectly acceptable to do so and if the funeral home, where your loved one is currently, tells you that they will need the transportation fee paid for, for picking granny up last night, you tell them that it is illegal for them to hold your grandma's body for ransom. Essentially that is what they are doing by telling you, "OK, you are welcome to go elsewhere, we just need the two-or three-hundred-dollar transport fee to cover the cost of picking her up last night." They cannot do that. If they wish to approach your chosen funeral home with that, they are welcome to do so. But if you choose to go elsewhere, you are able to do just that.

What? Oh, yes, that is a little something that these funeral homes don't want you to know. Especially the corporate ones. You are well within your rights to go elsewhere. The only caveat to this may be an existing preneed agreement that Granny signed years ago. It may be legally binding and require that payment. But essentially, just like every other place on the planet, if you don't want to do business with XYZ Funeral Home, you don't have to. Even Prearrangements are transferrable. It does not state on any pre-arrangement that you *must* do business with a particular funeral home. The money paid up front in a prearrangement agreement is placed in a policy of a third-party trust company. It is transferrable to pretty much any funeral home. The third party makes sure the funeral home gets paid.

If you don't like a restaurant, you walk out. If you cannot come to an agreement at the car dealer, you leave. If you know that TV you have your eye on is half-price at Walmart, you leave that huge appliance dealer and go to Walmart. This is how business is done, and burying or cremating your dear loved one is a business, just like any other; here, too, you can choose whom you do business with. You can go elsewhere.

Those questions I told you to ask? If you get an answer to any of those questions you don't like, you can go elsewhere. *You* are the customer at a funeral home. Not the deceased. You are the one whom will be paying the contract (Unless already taken care of by insurance or pre-arrangement). Either way, there may be incidentals you will have to pay for, such as obituaries, extra copies of death certificates, et cetera. But ultimately, the choice is yours. Choose wisely.

Now, don't get me wrong. I am not anticorporate! I know that there is another certainty in life beyond dying and paying taxes. That certainty is the fact that in this day, this age, if you are going to do business, more than likely, it will be with a big corporation. I buy from Amazon. I am a Walmart customer. I choose these corporations for what they can offer; usually it comes down to price and convenience. The two-day shipping through Amazon Prime really has me addicted, and I do so love the low, low price that Walmart and other major retail firms offer. It's all about supply and demand and the big boys can certainly buy up truckloads and in turn offer the prices that they do. It's business. I am, instead, bemoaning the fact of how the funeral industry is playing upon your grief and then, before you know it, quick as a flash, they have talked you into an elaborate, mostly overpriced, balm for that grief. There really is no other business like it, save for perhaps the medical industry and its becoming quite sleezy.

Today, in this country, we have become virtual sitting ducks when it comes to those services that we dearly need and the fact that when a sudden death occurs, we are trapped by those who claim they care. If you can't get that TV at the price you want, there will perhaps be a sale in the future. If you have your eye on that new Honda, you know to wait until the end of the year when you can get it at a lower price as dealerships are trying to make room for newer models. There are little tricks of the trade that you can take advantage of to get the best price. Black Friday happens for a reason, after all. But when that loved one dies, when they have taken their last breath, make no mistake. There is an industry, a major industry, that is banking on the fact that you need to do something with Grandma.

The major corporations I have mentioned in this book are out to make a buck. It is, after all, the American way. I don't fault them for simply doing business. I am however, asking and illustrating for you to be mindful of that smartly dressed funeral director. He is a salesman—period. He doesn't know what kind of person your loved one was. He doesn't have a horse in the race. He is simply there to make sure their send-off is done at the right price. Dignity and respect? They will use those words, but let's face it, those words are only important to you.

Mortuary schools and college programs are churning out funeral directors and licensing boards are granting licensure to those who want to make a living. They may get into this business for a variety of reasons, from "it's a family business" to "I want to help people." But at the end of the day, it is about making a living and if they can make a lucrative one, all the better. With that said, I have known some true professionals in this business. Those who really do care. I am not saying that the funeral business as a whole is full of money-grubbing boogeymen, not at all. What I am saying is, if large corporations continue to gobble up small hometown funeral establishments, employing price hikes and less-than-scrupulous sales tactics, then the business of "caring" becomes sullied indeed. Let's face it, there are very few old-fashioned town doctors anymore. There are few shade tree mechanics and good old hometown proprietors of small businesses. Major medical corporations and cars that are basically large computers have done away with these. The same is happening to your local undertaker.

That is why an honest, frank discussion about death, dying and final wishes needs to take place within families. Ask questions of your local funeral homes; meet with preneed specialists. Many of them are third-party contractors anyway and are out to make a buck as well, but ask questions of them. If you or your family is leaning toward cremation, ask questions about that too. Right now, there is an influx of "cremation societies" that send out mailers inviting you to have lunch and learn about the "peace of mind that comes with prearranging your cremation." They will dazzle you with numbers and tell you that they offer that sought after peace of mind. They will tell you they are well-established, many years of experience, yadda yadda. Truth be told, when all is said and done, you could be signing up for a simple cremation plan costing anywhere from $3000 to $5000 through an organization that contracts a third-party removal service to pick you up and crematories that are fifty or a hundred miles away to perform the cremation. Before you know it, four or five other entities have handled your departure from this earthly realm. There are direct disposers out there who will do it for a lot less and have their own facilities, and you can pre arrange with them as well.

Let me also touch very briefly on "green cremation." There is a new and environmentally friendly way to cremate. It is alkaline hydrolysis and it is becoming sort of a thing in larger communities. A regular cremation involves fire. A fire that burns close to two thousand degrees Fahrenheit. As we have discussed, after the cremation, bone material is swept from the chamber pulverized and given back as cremated remains. Hydrolysis uses a chemical compound to "speed up decomposition." Essentially, the deceased is placed in a large chamber, usually without any clothing or cover. A chemical is administered and the body is, um, essentially, um, chemically dissolved. If you are thinking it sounds gruesome, you may be right. It is being billed as "green cremation" or "an environmentally friendly cremation." Some places offer it and I am not here to say yay or nay; I have my opinions on it, but if it is offered to you as an option, I urge you to ask many, many questions and do your homework when considering. Hey, what the hell, google it. Alkaline hydrolysis. See for yourself. CANA (Cremation Association of North America) has some writings on the topic. Take a look at that. As far as cost, it also may cost more than regular cremation.

The point here is, if at all possible, do your homework. Arrange a preneed meeting. Meet with your local funeral home. Ask questions. In the area I live in, there are about ten funeral homes and five of them are corporate. There are also four direct disposers and only one of those is corporate-owned. So have that discussion with your family and decide for yourself. If you feel comfortable with a corporate-owned funeral home, then go for it. Just know, going in, that sometimes—sometimes—the locally owned and operated establishment, one with a track record of serving families in your community, may be the way to go. Don't let a knee-jerk last-minute decision trap you somewhere that may be simply out for the contents of your wallet and nothing more.

There are even little things you can do now to lessen the cost when the time comes. Buy your urn now. Google "cremation urns for sale." You will find some really cool ones. Buy your casket ahead of time. Yep, you can find those too. That is, if you have the storage space for such an object. I know it sounds macabre, and every now and then there is a local news reporter who trots out to some guy's house who decided to do just that. It's funny. It's unique. "Hey, this guy bought a Budweiser casket! He has it in his basement. It is what he wants to be buried in it when he goes, isn't that a hoot!" Yep, it's crazy, crazy like a fox! Funeral homes hate when you do stuff like that. It means they won't get to sell you that marked-up merchandise. Trust me, you can find everything you need merchandise-wise for when you or your lived one's time comes.

Let me also say, as this book nears its end, that it is not all bad. There are dedicated people who work in the industry. From the hospice nurse who holds the hand of that person whose family is not around to that funeral professional that truly does care, there are people out there still dedicated to this difficult work. There are those too who speak and counsel and console on the topic of grief. When you cannot find the strength to get out of bed because one you loved so dearly has gone, there are those resources that will help you make sense of it and continue to live. This is why I say, do your research.

Corporations will do their thing. They will go after your money and I honestly do not think that these words I have written will change that. However, there are those caring, concerned professionals out there who will make a most painful experience a little more, well, tolerable. Find *those* people. Do business with *those* people. They still exist. Corporate has taken their eye off the ball and it doesn't have to be the way it has become.

CHAPTER 15

I Lied

When I started this book—I wrote as much in my forward—
I set out to set the record straight about myself. I said that
this in no way was a literary middle finger to my past employer, nor
was I out to do any financial harm to any particular organization. I
lied. The way business is done today in the funeral industry I certainly do raise a hearty middle finger to, and yes, I aim to do some
damage. OK, perhaps damage is not an appropriate term. I aim to,
let's say, shake things up a bit.

We have established that people are fascinated by death and
there are people who work in the many facets of the after-care or
death-care business who got into the business for the right reasons
but remain in it for the wrong ones. Quite frankly, there are those
in this industry that really and truly should consider other lines of
employment. From the funeral director who views you as nothing
more than a big payday to the foul and indifferent, there are those
who really truly need to get out of the business altogether. Corporations have most assuredly taken this industry into a high-pressure
sales-pitch atmosphere, and they have hardened funeral staff and
done irreparable damage.

I mentioned previously that I had my own "awakening." When
I started to care about nothing more than the numbers, how many I
could do and I saw my own sense of caring start to erode, then I got

out. There is a lot I miss about the business. I was extremely good at my job and took it very seriously. I cared until I stopped caring, and then, and only then, was it clear to me that I was becoming that which I hated.

Are corporations the death knell (pun) to the funeral business? Certainly not. They have a unique opportunity to really offer that service of caring on a very large scale. But it has to be about the *people*! As long as they continue to raise prices without good reason, as long as they continue to pressure their staff into selling everything from little mementos to DNA sampling to little tchotchkes and marking up inferior products all in the name of profit, then that service of caring becomes little more than a glamorized sales-pitch from some carnival barker in a suit and tie.

This book has been more about me than anything else. I recognized the fact a long time ago that I have a bit of an ego. Most writers do. I made no bones (just look at all these funeral puns) about the fact that I was in the entertainment business. However, when I got into the funeral business it was during a time that I desperately needed to get rid of me! I needed to do something for others and I needed to work in a business where I was *not* the most important person in the room and one where I felt I was truly helping make a difference. I felt that I did that in my time in the industry. I also felt after some time that I was perhaps the only one who felt that way. I have cremated family, friends and acquaintances. I took it as an honor and still do. But death and the industry it is becoming were really wearing on me.

Take heed. There is a multi-billion-dollar industry out there that is waiting and relying upon your grief. It is an industry that employs some people who will hand you tissues while they grasp at your credit card. I simply write these words to warn you not to play into their trap. Read your contract, if you really don't think an item is necessary, don't purchase it. You are in charge. Get a trusted friend or family member to go with you and to advise when you feel overwhelmed. It is a difficult time and if you're not careful you will pay way too much. They are counting on that.

Years ago, when my wife of twenty years passed, I spiraled into a dark fog. I could hardly function, I could hardly breathe. There were so many emotions. I didn't know what to do or how to do it. But I did know the business and knew how it worked and one thing became certain: I did not want to go through a corporate funeral home. Geographically, I was in an area where I knew no one and was unfamiliar with the funeral establishments in that area. It all seems like a blur now, but I did have the wherewithal to decide on a well-established family-run funeral home. That was my decision and I regret nothing about it and met with some very professional and, I feel, honorable people. But there I was, in a situation I did not see coming. I had to decide. I did. It helped that I knew the business. Even while making the arrangements, I was offered a job. Funny now, looking back.

The point is, I spent much of my fifteen years in the funeral business in a non-corporate establishment and then spent some time in the corporate world of the funeral industry. Mistakes, miscommunication and things I have mentioned in this book will happen. But I truly feel that when you take your eyes off the ball (people, caring, compassion) and start worrying about the bottom line of the ledger, then the mistakes will become innumerable, commonplace and— really—no one will give a damn. The money all spends the same.

I had to leave. Not because I hated my job, not because I hated the people. I had to leave because I hated me. I no longer cared. I no longer wanted to care. I mean, that wasn't my job, was it? No, in the big business of death, it is not your job to care. That is what I came to discover. When I started years ago, I could hardly work a funeral service without tearing up. Now I had become this unfeeling, uncaring, calloused thing who I no longer recognized; I knew something had to change. So, with no fanfare, and after all those years in the business, I left. My colleagues had no parting words for me, nothing to say, not even a goodbye. Hmm. Perhaps it was not just me who hated me. It was time to leave.

By the way, Amazon has great prices on Caskets and Urns.